Online Education Comes of Age: Schools for the Future

Also from Westphalia Press
westphaliapress.org

The Idea of the Digital University

France and New England Volumes 1, 2, & 3

Treasures of London

The History of Photography

L'Enfant and the Freemasons

Baronial Bedrooms

Making Trouble for Muslims

Material History and Ritual Objects

Paddle Your Own Canoe

Opportunity and Horatio Alger

Careers in the Face of Challenge

Bookplates of the Kings

Collecting American Presidential Autographs

Freemasonry in Old Buffalo

Young Freemasons?

Social Satire and the Modern Novel

The Essence of Harvard

Ivanhoe Masonic Quartettes

A Definitive Commentary on Bookplates

James Martineau and Rebuilding Theology

No Bird Lacks Feathers

Gilded Play

Earthworms, Horses, and Living Things

The Man Who Killed President Garfield

Anti-Masonry and the Murder of Morgan

Understanding Art

Homeopathy

Fishing the Florida Keys

Collecting Old Books

Masonic Secret Signs and Passwords

The Thomas Starr King Dispute

Earl Warren's Masonic Lodge

Lariats and Lassos

Mr. Garfield of Ohio

The Wisdom of Thomas Starr King

The French Foreign Legion

War in Syria

Naturism Comes to the United States

New Sources on Women and Freemasonry

Designing, Adapting, Strategizing in Online Education

Gunboat and Gun-runner

Meeting Minutes of Naval Lodge No. 4 F.A.A.M

Online Education Comes of Age: Schools for the Future

Volume 4, Number 2 of Internet Learning

Edited by Melissa Layne

WESTPHALIA PRESS
An imprint of Policy Studies Organization

Online Education Comes of Age: Schools for the Future: Volume 4, Number 2 of Internet Learning
All Rights Reserved © 2015 by Policy Studies Organization

Westphalia Press
An imprint of Policy Studies Organization
1527 New Hampshire Ave., NW
Washington, D.C. 20036
info@ipsonet.org

ISBN-13: 978-1-63391-753-8
ISBN-10: 1-63391-753-3

Cover design by Jeffrey Barnes:
www.jbarnesbook.design

Daniel Gutierrez-Sandoval, Executive Director
PSO and Westphalia Press

Updated material and comments on this edition
can be found at the Westphalia Press website:
www.westphaliapress.org

Internet Learning Journal
Volume 4, Number 2 - Fall 2015
© 2015 Policy Studies Organization
ipsonet.org/publications/open-access/internet-learning

Table of Contents

Letter from the Editor_____3
Melissa Layne

Editors and Editorial Board_____5

Meeting the Holistic Needs of K-12 Online Learners: Designing Schools for the Future_____7
Sarah Bryans-Bongey, Nevada State College

The Future of mLearning Begins with a Baseline Pedagogy_____25
Elizabeth Cook, American Public University System

Employee Motivations for Workplace Learning and the Role of Elearning in the Workplace_____37
Jason G. Caudill, King University

3 Questions for an Online Leader_____49
Featuring Phil Ice

The Tangible and Intangible Benefits of Offering Massive Open Online Courses: Faculty Perspectives_____52
Credence Baker, Tarleton State University, Fred Nafukho, Texas A&M University, Karen McCaleb, Texas A&M Corpus Christi, Melissa Becker, Tarleton State University, and Michelle Johnson, Texas A&M University

The Intersection of Exemplar Professional Accreditation Standards and Quality Matters Rubric Standards for Best Practice in Distance Education_____69
Nancy E. Krusen, Pacific University

Gamification Challenges and a Case Study in Online Learning_____82
Darren Wilson, Colorado Technical University, Cynthia Calongne, Colorado Technical University, and Brook Henderson, American Public University

Advanced Faculty Professional Development for Online Course Building: An Action Research Project_____103
Philip Aust, Griselda Thomas, Tamara Powell, Christopher K. Randall, Vanessa Slinger-Friedman, Joe Terantino, and Tiffani Reardon, Kennesaw State University

Letter from the Editor
Dr. Melissa Layne, Ed.D.

Fall 2015 Issue

Without a doubt, this fall has been one of the busiest, as we continue to see our *Internet Learning Journal* readership and author submissions grow. These increasing numbers are a testament to our excellent marketing team, promotional efforts at conferences, invited webinars, workshops, and meetings with other university leaders outside of APUS. It's been an absolute pleasure talking to people inside and outside of academe and sharing the evolution of our journal—from our humble beginnings of a print and web-based publication to a multi-platform and interactive scholarly publication. That said, the impetus behind this transformation has not been openly shared…until now.

On my way back from a recent trip to South Africa (and consequently having several hours of flight time), I picked up the airline-hosted magazine, *Sawubona*--which in the Zulu language translates to "*Hello*" or "*Good day.*" I always like flipping through this particular magazine during my trips over because it is a wonderful collection of articles on just about everything---food and wine, business, sports, lifestyle, leisure, art, fashion--and of course my favorite topic…technology. So on this flight, instead of opening up to the beginning, I cheated and went straight to the technology section article entitled "*Generation Z: the digital game-changers*" and knew right away I was in for a treat.

Although I was already somewhat familiar with the newest kids on the block (dubbed Gen Z-ers), the author of this article describes them in candid detail. They bear no resemblance to the Millennial generation, nor are they like any other generation that begat them. Here are just a few of Dion Chang's (author)
observations on Gen Z-ers. They
- range in age from 13-17
- are online researchers
- are extremely creative
- are realists
- live in a world of cyberspace and their toys are videos and mobile platforms
- are adaptive
- are visual communicators (emoticons and emojis)

Toward the end of the article, he summarizes their world as one of "start-up entrepreneurship, new apps (daily), customization, on-demand everything and making their own pocket money from YouTube." I was so fascinated by this article, I believe I've read it at least 5 or 6 times thus far.

doi: 10.18278/il.4.2.1

What makes this short piece so fascinating is that *we* (collectively as academics and researchers) have this information at our fingertips, yet the ways in which online teaching and learning is currently being delivered at most educational institutions is a far cry from what this up-and-coming demographic will expect in terms of content delivery. Many of us have missed the mark by only focusing on what current tech gadgets or apps they are using, but have not stopped to consider Gen Zs' *other* diverse characteristics, nor are we asking probing questions as to *why* they use Snapchat and Instagram over Facebook, for example. Believe it or not, they view failure as a badge of honor; an opportunity to grow and improve--and to be quite blunt, we should be doing the same. Are we ready for this pragmatism? Some of us will be ready, but the reality is that many of us will not.

Well, I have to say that much of our inspiration for heading down this unpaved road with the *Internet Learning Journal* comes from the Generation Z-ers. Although I was born a few generations before Gen Z, I admire many of their intriguing attributes and downright "take no prisoners" attitude, hence my fervor behind changing the journal into something interactive and engaging for our readers. We have been determined to "talk the talk" and "walk the walk" by refusing to publish scholarly work using age-old processes only to produce something that is dense, and boring to read. We want to our readers to have an *experience* after engaging with the rich "stories" that our scholars have worked so diligently to publish. On that note, I'm very excited to present the work of our authors in this issue who share the same passion for curiosity and creativity. If you haven't already perused our interactive versions of the journal, I encourage you to do so by going to the *App Store* on Apple tablets and phones, or *Google Play* on Android tablets and phones, search for the free app *Internet Learning Journal*, and download.

On behalf of all of us at *Internet Learning Journal*, we would like to thank you, our readers, for your continued support.

Happy Holidays!

Dr. Melissa Layne
Editor-in-Chief for *Internet Learning Journal*

Editors and Editorial Board

Editor-in-Chief Melissa Layne, *American Public University System*

Associate Editors Paul Rich, *Policy Studies Organization*
Phil Ice, *American Public University System*
Samantha Adams-Becker, *New Media Consortium*
Julie Schell, *University of Texas-Austin*
Daniel Benjamin, *American Public University System*
Carol Hrusovsky, *Hondros College*
Chuck Dziuban, *University of Central Florida*
Mark Milliron, *Civitas Learning*
Holly Henry, *American Public University System*

Managing Editor Daniel Sandoval Guitterez, *Policy Studies Organization*

Editorial Board

Patricia Campbell, *American Public University System*
Lev Gonick, *Case Western Reserve University*
Kitayu Marre, *University of Dayton*
Gary Miller, *Penn State University*
Burks Oakley III, *University of Illinois*
Tony Picciano, *City University of New York*
Boria Sax, *Mercy College*
Peter Shea, *State University of New York at Albany*
Karen Swan, *University of Illinois*
Ellen Wager, *WCET*
Tony Mays, *South African Institute Distance Education*
Lynn Wright, *American Public University System*
Sarah Canfield Fuller, *American Public University System*
Paul Prinsloo, *University of South Africa*
Ngoni Chipere, *University of the West Indies*
Tony Onwuegbuzie, *Sam Houston State University*
Molly M. Lim, *American Public University System*
Clark Quinn, *Quinnovation*
Ben W. Betts, *University of Warwick, UK*
Mike Howarth, *Middlesex University*
Tarek Zoubir, *Middlesex University*
Jackie Hee Young Kim, *Armstrong Atlantic State University*
Hannah R. Gerber, *Sam Houston State University*
Debra P. Price, *Sam Houston State University*
Mauri Collins, *St. Rebel Design, LLC*
Ray Schroeder, *University of Illinois Springfield*
Don Olcott, Jr., *HJ Global*
Kay Shattuck, *Quality Matters and Penn State University*
Karan Powell, *American Public University System*
John Sener, *Senerknowledge LLC*
Melissa Langdon, *University of Notre Dame, Australia*
Kristen Betts, *Drexel University*
Barbara Altman, *Texas A&M, Central Texas Associates*
Herman van der Merwe, *North-West University Vaal Triangle Campus*
Robert Rosenbalm, *Dallas County Community College District*
Carmen Elena Cirnu, *National Institute for Research & Development in Informatics, Bucharest*
Beverly Irby, *Texas A & M University*
Fred Nafukho, *Texas A & M University*
Ron Callahan, *School of Visual Arts, New York*
Adam Bulizak, *Hondros College*

Meeting the Holistic Needs of K-12 Online Learners: Designing Schools for the Future

Sarah Bryans-Bongey[A]

Introduction

According to the annual report, *Keeping Pace with K-12 Digital Learning* (Watson, Pape, Murin, Gemin, & Vashaw, 2014), the total number of K-12 students attending online school programs continues to climb. In 2013-2014, student enrollment in K-12 online programs increased by 6.2%. As of 2014, 30 U.S. states had fully online K-12 schools (Watson et al., 2014). Many online schools and programs provide educational programs to students at all levels of K-12 education. In the *Keeping Pace* report's section "National Snapshot of Online Learning Activity," Alabama, Arkansas, Florida, Michigan, and Virginia have established online learning requirements for grades 9-12 students, and a large majority of the state programs with fully online programs also offer programming for students in elementary and/or middle school grades (Watson, et al, 2014).

This information is impressive, and the sheer growth in numbers might imply an unequivocal success story relating to the overall increase in student enrollments in K-12 online teaching and learning. However, despite the fact that new students come into online programs in rapidly increasing numbers, existing students are simultaneously switching from one online program to another, or they may be leaving the online program universe altogether. In higher education, this phenomenon is called "swirling" (Layne, Boston, and Ice, 2013).

Review of the Literature

As is the case with online programs in higher education, the National Education Policy Center (Miron & Urschel, 2012) observed this high rate of attrition in its study of the nation's largest K-12 online school provider, and urged continued and "careful study of various aspects of full-time virtual schools," with the goal being "to help ensure that full-time virtual schools can better serve students and the public as a whole" (para. 2). More research

---

[A] **Sarah Bryans-Bongey**, Ed.D. is Assistant Professor of Education, and coordinator of the educational technology endorsement at Nevada State College (NSC). Dr. Bryans-Bongey's research interests include web-enhanced, blended, and online learning, educational technology integration, Universal Design for Learning (UDL), and student engagement. Her research on UDL and teaching with technology has led to various publications and presentations. She is co-editor of *Online Teaching in K-12: Models, Methods, and Best Practices for Teachers and Administrators* (Information Today, Inc.: in press).

doi: 10.18278/il.4.2.2

is needed to determine the reasons for online student attrition and, similarly, more research is needed to identify successful strategies for boosting retention rates in online programs. Despite the impressive overall increase in K-12 students coming to online learning, some state virtual schools are actually shrinking, and others have not shown enrollment growth for two years in a row (Watson, et. al, 2014).

There is limited information as to the exact cause of the swirling phenomenon. Some suggest it is logistically and physically easier for students to drop one program and start another when the programs are virtual as opposed to being offered in a physical or location-bound environment. Trial enrollment or enrollment in a program based on a temporary situation such as illness or injury may explain some of the fluxuation in the enrollment of K-12 students in online programs. Considering the findings of Layne, Boston, and Ice (2013), additional causes for online students to become swirlers could arise from challenges of the student to locate an online program that is compatible with his or her needs and interests. Also, the latest generation of K-12 students – Gen Z – is known to consist of shoppers with a growing influence in household spending. This youngest generation of learners has been dubbed the "digital game changers" (Chang, 2015, September). In examining the swirling phenomenon and the suggestion that 'demographic predictors' may be relevant (Layne, et al., 2013), the observation that Gen Z demonstrates less brand loyalty, a strong influence on household spending, and a shopper mentality may be factors to consider when planning and designing online programs for K-12.

> **Despite the impressive overall increase in K-12 students coming to online learning, some state virtual schools are actually shrinking, and others have not shown enrollment growth for two years in a row** (Watson, et. al, 2014).

Models and Methods to Measure Online Student Engagement and Retention: Applications at the Course and Program Level

Extracurricular activities such as clubs and sports are not technically considered to be a requirement of public K-12 education. Some educators and policymakers suggest addressing social or holistic aspects of student development is not a priority for programs, administrators, or teachers involved with K-12 public education, regardless of the format. However, a report from the National Center for Education Statistics (NCES, 1995; 2012) found that "participation in extracurricular activities may increase students' sense of engagement" (para. 1). According to the NCES report, "If indeed, participation in extracurricular activities can lead to success in school, then the availability of these activities to students of all backgrounds becomes an important equity issue" (NCES, 1995, para. 1). At the program-wide level, both private and public K-12 online programs are continuing to create, explore, and evaluate ways to engage learners through social and extracurricular activities. The body of research continues to grow, and this report begins to explore the nature and prevalence of this type of enrichment in K-12 online programs. Below are some additional survey instruments used to measure perceptual student engagement, involvement, and retention.

National Survey of Student Engagement (NSSE)

On-going research from the National Survey of Student Engagement (NSSE) suggests that when students are involved in their school they are more likely to be satisfied, engaged, and successful. "Participation in extracurricular activities…and conversations with faculty and peers have been positively related to persistence and satisfaction" (Kuh, 1995, p. 124). While Kuh's (1995) early research and perspectives on retention pertain to the face-to-face (f2f) college environment, it can be seen in this study that practitioners and professionals in the field of K-12 online learning have begun to explore and apply likely approaches to engage and support students enrolled in K-12 online programs.

> "Participation in extracurricular activities…and conversations with faculty and peers have been positively related to persistence and satisfaction"
> (Kuh, 1995, p. 124).

The High School Survey of Student Engagement (HSSSE)

The High School Survey of Student Engagement (HSSSE) suggests similar connections between opportunities for involvement and student retention and success, and cites an "engagement gap" in which girls are more engaged than boys and white and Asian students are more engaged than students of other backgrounds (Yazzie-Mintz, 2009, 2010). While highlighting gaps in engagement, the authors of the HSSSE report also state that "the primary focus and goal of public schools is student achievement" as measured by outcomes, test scores, graduation rates, and annual yearly progress (Yazzie-Mintz, 2010, para. 1).

Community of Inquiry Survey

When considering online programs offered at the course level, the Community of Inquiry (CoI) model (Garrison, Anderson, & Archer, 2001) suggests that courses are likely to support higher levels of student engagement and success when they address holistic attributes that go beyond an emphasis on quality course content alone. The CoI model (see *Figure 1* below) describes essential elements of social, cognitive, and teaching presence. When working in concert these three elements are seen to have a positive impact on the satisfaction and retention of online students (Boston, Diaz, Gibson, Ice, Richardson, and Swan, 2009; Garrison, Anderson, & Archer, 2001; Garrison, 2011). At a more programmatic level, the NSSE and the HSSSE can assist in determining how various opportunities for student involvement affects student retention.

The Community of Inquiry (CoI) survey, The National Survey of Student Engagement (NSSE) and the High School Survey of Student Engagement (HSSSE) explore specific attributes, structures, and frameworks contributing to student retention and success, and therefore have relevance to those seeking to measure these elements in an online school setting.

Purpose of the Study

In this pilot study, basic attitudes and program structures among teachers and administrators of K-12 online classes and programs are explored. Existing elements

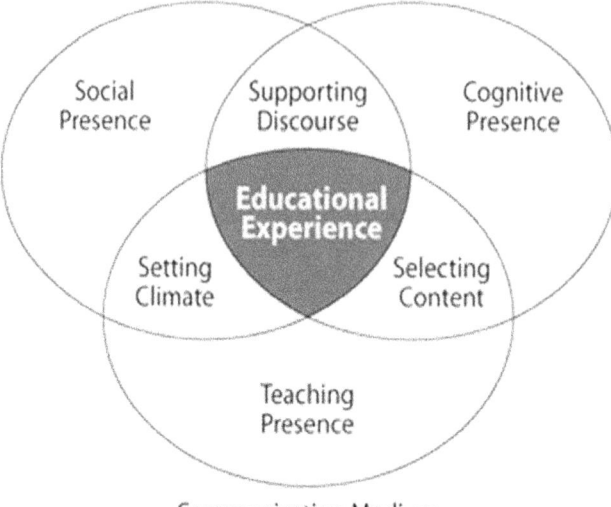

Figure 1. CoI Model.

found in the CoI, as well as the NSSE and HSSSE studies, are examined in an attempt to identify *if* and *how* such elements are being valued and implemented in a K-12 online courses and programs.

Drawing from information provided by anonymous survey respondents and professional members of the International Association for K-12 Online Learning (iNACOL) organization, the results from this study identify and share approaches that K-12 online programs and professionals are currently using to meet the holistic and social needs of students as part of their online schooling.

Methodology

Participants and Setting

Respondents to this survey were 31 professionals and practitioner-members of the iNACOL. Respondents were predominantly teachers and principals, but also included specialists, school development directors, university faculty, and other administrators and supervisors from online schools across the country. Twenty-five (83%) of the 31 survey respondents worked in institutions offering high school-level programs, 21 (70%) were affiliated with online middle school programs, and 10 (33%) described strategies and experiences relating to elementary-level programming. There was some overlap, with the likelihood that some people may be working in programs that support multiple grades/levels. Two of the respondents were not directly or currently affiliated with a specific online school or program.

Instrument and Procedures

The development of specific survey questions involved the inclusion of common extracurricular and enrichment activities found in K-12 schools and also the consideration of questions included on the NSSE (NSSE, 2015).

A mixed methods approach was used, with question types including 11 multiple choice questions and three questions that sought a qualitative response on most popular programs, student responses to the programs, and the non-academic programs that seem most useful to the survey respondent. Little is known about the types of co-curricular, extra-curricular, and holistic programs and supports in place in online schools. Therefore, the focus was simply to get an initial idea of whether and how such holistic and enrichment activities were being implemented and teacher/administrator perspectives as to their importance. Please see Appendix A for a complete list of survey questions.

The survey was distributed by iNACOL on behalf of the researcher. The survey was distributed in May, 2015, with a summary report posted on the iNACOL Research Forum in June of 2015. The survey was distributed to all iNACOL members who subscribed to the General Discussion forum.

Analysis

Although the sample is too small to make this data generalizable, it is clear that the 31 professionals and experts participating in this mixed-methods research had strong feelings (either pro or con) regarding the need for holistic programs and extra-curricular socialization and enrichment.

The types of extracurricular, social and community options explored can be tied back to the types of questions included on the NSSE. Quantitative responses to an array of possible activities and supports gave insight into the frequency of various practices in K-12 online programs, and the provision of opportunities for open-ended responses and comments allowed respondents to share additional information and add individual attitudes, innovations, and concerns to the discussion. The qualitative responses elicited in this fashion were categorized as positive or negative, with one person responding negatively about the concept of addressing social needs, and making the point that often such students are seeking to remove themselves from the social awkwardness and bullying that they may have experienced in a f2f classroom. Fourteen survey participants did not respond to the open-ended question.

Results

Results revealed practical strategies for engaging students in an online school community. Approaches included fully online as well as blended and f2f opportunities to collaborate and augment the academic and asynchronous life of the online school. After this research peeks into the frequency with which online programs are incorporating such approaches, a logical next question (not addressed here) is do they help? At the time of this writing, there was no Online Survey of Student Engagement. It should be noted that the survey results reflect responses from the individual anonymous respondents and do not necessarily reflect the opinion or position of the iNACOL organization itself.

A surprise that may suggest strong variation in the philosophy and function of the different online schools represented was the fact that no one was neutral on the question of whether K-12 students need programs in support of social and emotional development. The questions from the survey were not designed to request that respondents identify their affiliation according to public versus private school interests. However, this may be an influential factor worthy of further exploration in a future study.

Table 1
Respondent Attitudes Regarding the Importance of Programming for Social and Emotional Development

Level of Agreement	Number Responding	Percentage
Strongly Agree	13	42%
Agree	11	35%
Neither Agree nor Disagree	0	0%
Disagree	1	3%
Strongly Disagree	6	19%

Table 2
Descriptive Statistics

Statistics	
Min Value	1
Max Value	5
Mean	3.77
Variance	2.31
Standard Deviation	1.52
Total Responses	31

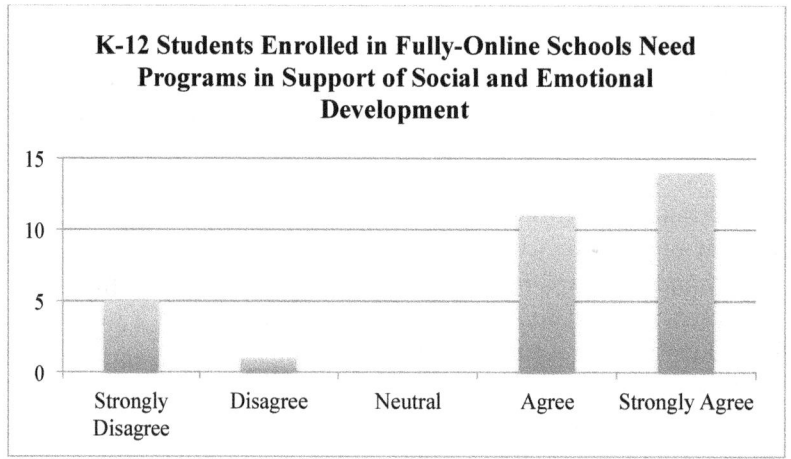

Figure 1. Respondent attitudes on the provision of programming to support K-12 online students in their social and emotional development.

The data shown in Tables 1 and 2 reveal respondent attitudes in terms of how strongly they agree or disagree that online students need programs that support them in their social and emotional development.

Many survey respondents noted the existence of non-academic programs to support students in their programs. Items mentioned as being beneficial included a list of items that included field trips, city-wide project collaboration, social work groups, peer mentoring, involvement with the local newspaper, a spiritual life group, an online talent show, and other activities. Fewer than half of the survey respondents (15/31) answered the qualitative question about non-academic programs provided to online students, and one of 15 people who did respond provided an alternate viewpoint by stating that "families enroll their K-12 children in online schools to get away from the 'socialization' of public schools. It's brutal to stand in line in the hall, get bullied, be lonely on the playground, etc." This emphasizes that not all professionals and practitioners are convinced that social or non-academic programs are needed or desired by students and families involved in K-12 online education.

The majority of respondents (69.44%) felt that the best delivery methods for non-academic student supports would be as a combination of both online and f2f approaches. The second most common response was from programs that used fully online approaches only, with some respondents commenting that f2f events were not practical due to circumstances of the program (e.g., the large range covered by the online school or other transportation-related issues). In considering non-academic student supports that are practical and desirable, the five most commonly cited activities reported by all respondents were service projects, clubs, field trips, orientation events, and social gatherings.

Orientations were offered by most of the programs, and some respondents commented that these were mandatory. As shown in Table 3, many of the orientation events involved f2f as well as online elements. Activities that seem to have the highest level of online-only distribution included clubs, showcases of student work, and exercise.

A large proportion of the respondents also described efforts to involve parents, guardians, and community members. When asked to identify any adult-led groups or individuals that promote and enrich the school community, 11 respondents reported the inclusion of parents or community members as guest speakers. A number of people reported the presence of a Parent Teacher Association, and also noted that parents were involved in field trips, fundraising activities, and special events. Tables 4 and 5 below show details, including specific nature of web meetings and f2f events.

> "families enroll their K-12 children in online schools to get away from the 'socialization' of public schools. It's brutal to stand in line in the hall, get bullied, be lonely on the playground, etc."

Conclusion

These data represent attitudes and information from professionals working across 20-31 different K-12 online programs nationwide. The goal of this study was to seek answers to questions about social and non-academic supports, and what these supports may look like in

Table 3
Response Rates on Student Enrichment/Supports by Format and Category

#	Question	Online Only	Face-to-Face Only	Both Online and Face-to-Face	Not Applicable	Total Responses	Mean
1	Social Gatherings	2	3	15	2	22	2.77
2	Field Trips	1	6	9	5	21	2.86
4	Exercise	8	2	5	5	20	2.35
5	Recreational Events	0	7	7	6	20	2.95
6	Cultural Enrichment	7	1	7	6	21	2.57
7	Service Projects	4	5	9	3	21	2.52
8	Dances	0	10	2	7	19	2.84
9	End of Year Celebration	0	10	6	5	21	2.76
10	Holiday Events (religious)	0	0	0	15	15	4.00
11	Holiday Events (non-sectarian)	1	4	1	11	17	3.29
12	Orientation Events	7	5	10	0	22	2.14
14	Other (please explain)	0	0	1	9	10	3.90
15	Showcases of Student Work	8	0	13	2	23	2.39
16	Clubs	8	4	9	2	23	2.22
17	Special Interest Groups	6	2	8	5	21	2.57

Table 4
Adult individuals or groups that promote and enrich the school community

#	Answer	Response	%
1	Parent Teacher Association (PTA)	7	41.18%
2	Parent Fundraising Events	3	17.65%
3	Parents involved in Virtual of F2F Field Trips	7	41.18%
4	Parents or Community Members as Guest Speakers	11	64.71%
5	Web Meetings (please explain)	3	17.65%
6	Face-to-Face Events (please explain)	6	35.29%
7	Click to write Choice 7	1	5.88%

Table 5
Explanations of Face-to-Face and Web-based Events

Web Meetings (please explain)	Face-to-Face Events (please explain)
School assembly	Monthly outings
Virtual field trips	We have Regional Area Coordinators who plan events for students in their area.
	Orientations and Open Houses
	Student Council
	Interviewing Practice, Club events

a subset of K-12 online school programs. Research on a broad scale is required to measure the impact of social and non-academic programs on K-12 online student engagement, retention, and success. These efforts can build upon theoretical foundations established in higher education such as the CoI model (Garrison, 2011; Garrison et al., 2001) and the work of NSSE (Kuh, 1996).

As innovations in instructional formats and school infrastructures continue to be implemented, program developers, policy makers, teachers, and administrators look beyond the big data of K-12 online growth and use technological opportunity to redefine education in positive and responsive ways. Research is needed in many areas of online teaching and learning. Guided by both data and imagination, it will be possible to craft, implement, evaluate, and refine new and innovative instructional models that will enrich and redefine K-12 education in the 21st century.

References

Boston, W., Diaz, S., Gibson, A. M., Ice, P., Richardson, J., & Swan, K. (2009). An exploration of the relationship between indicators of the community of inquiry framework and retention in online programs. *Journal of Asynchronous Learning Networks, 13*(3), 67-83. Retrieved from onlinelearningconsortium.org/sites/default/files/v13n3_8boston.pdf

Chang, D. (September, 2015). "Generation Z: The digital game changers." *Sawubona*, page 20.

Garrison, D. R. (2011). *Elearning in the 21st century: A framework for research and practice* (2nd ed.). New York, NY: Taylor and Francis.

Garrison, D. R., Anderson, T., & Archer, W. (2001). Critical inquiry in a text-based environment: Computer conferencing in higher education. *The Internet and Higher Education, 2*(2-3), 87-105.

Kuh, G. D. (1995). The other curriculum: Out-of-class experiences associated with student learning and personal development. *Journal of Higher Education, 66*(2), 123-155.

Layne, M., Boston, W. E., & Ice, P. (2013). A longitudinal study of online learners: Shoppers, swirlers, stoppers, and succeeders as a function of demographic characteristics. *Online Journal of Distance Learning Administration, 16*(2).

Miron, G., & Urschel, J. (2012). *Understanding and improving full-time virtual schools.* Retrieved from http://nepc.colorado.edu/publication/understanding-improving-virtual

National Center for Education Statistics. (1995). *Extracurricular participation and student engagement* (NCES 95-741). Retrieved from http://nces.ed.gov/pubs95/web/95741.asp

National Center for Education Statistics. (2012). *Higher Education: Gaps in Access and Persistence* (NCES 2012-046). Retrieved from https://nces.ed.gov/pubs2012/2012046/chapter3.asp

National Survey of Student Engagement (NSSE). (2015). *Survey Instrument.* Retrieved from http://nsse.indiana.edu/html/survey_instruments.cfm?Flag=yes&sy=2015

Swan, K., & Ice, P. (2010). The community of inquiry framework ten years later: Introduction to the special issue. *The Internet and Higher Education, 13*(1-2), 1-4.

Watson, J., Pape, L., Murin, A., Gemin, B., & Vashaw, L. (2014). *Keeping pace with K-12 digital online learning.* Grand Rapids, MI: Evergreen Education Group.

Yazzie-Mintz, E. (2009). *Engaging the voices of students: A report on the 2007 & 2008 High School Survey of Student Engagement.* Bloomington, IN: Center for Evaluation & Education Policy. Retrieved from http://www.indiana.edu/~ceep/hssse/images/HSSSE_2009_Report.pdf

Yazzie-Mintz, E. (2010). *Charting the path from engagement to achievement: A report on the 2009 High School Survey of Student Engagement.* Bloomington, IN: Center for Evaluation & Education Policy. Retrieved from http://ceep.indiana.edu/hssse/images/HSSSE_2010_Report.pdf

Definitions and Abbreviations

Blended	A combination or blend of both online and face-to-face approaches. Courses that take a blended approach to learning are also referred to as *hybrid*.
CoI	Community of Inquiry – The CoI is the first model developed for online teaching and learning. It describes three dynamic components or "presences" that work together to yield an engaging and effective learning environment.
f2f	face-to-face – Instruction or teaching and learning experiences that take place synchronously in the built environment are considered to be face-to-face.
Generation Z	Generation Z consists of digital natives who are approximately 13-17 years of age. They are realistic, creative, and hyper-connected to the digital world.
HSSSE	High School Survey of Student Achievement – Building on similar goals as the NSSE survey of students in higher education, the HSSSE is the High School Survey of Student Engagement, with the goal being to research extra- co-curricular and other high school activities and track if and how a higher level of engagement leads to student retention and success.
iNACOL	International Association for K-12 Online Learning - This international organization advocates for and promotes research and community around the practice of online teaching and learning.

NSSE The NSSE is a National Survey of Student Engagement. It was developed to explore the connections between student opportunities and engagement and student persistence and success.
http://nsse.indiana.edu/html/high_impact_practices.cfm

Swirlers This term originated in the higher education setting to describe the large number of students who switch from one online program to another or who leave online programs altogether. Despite the fact that K-12 online enrollments are showing an overall annual increase, the fact that some state virtual schools are actually shrinking suggests swirling is an emerging concern in K-12 online programs.

Appendix A. Survey of iNACOL members

1. Please identify your role in K-12 online teaching and learning

    ○ Counselor
    ○ Teacher
    ○ Principal
    ○ Superintendent
    ○ Other (please explain _____)

2. K-12 students who are enrolled in fully online schools need programs that will support them in their social and emotional development.

    ○ Strongly Disagree
    ○ Disagree
    ○ Neither Agree nor Disagree
    ○ Agree
    ○ Strongly Agree

Demographics

3. Grades served by online program (please check all that apply).

    ☐ High School (Grades 9-12)
    ☐ Middle School (Grades 6-8)
    ☐ Elementary (Grades 3-5)
    ☐ Primary (Grades K-2)
    ☐ Other

What is the name of the institution you are affiliated with? (optional)

4. Is your online school religiously affiliated?

○ Yes
○ No

5. Which of the following non-academic student supports are practical and desirable to implement (select all that apply):

☐ Social Gatherings
☐ Field Trips
☐ Recreational Events
☐ Cultural Enrichment
☐ Service Projects
☐ Dances
☐ End of Year Celebration
☐ Holiday Events (religious)
☐ Holiday Events (non-sectarian)
☐ Orientation Events
☐ Clubs
☐ Special Interest Groups
☐ Other (please explain)

6. Thinking of your own online school/program, which is the best delivery method for programming designed to promote social/emotional development and a sense of community among K-12 online learners.

○ Online activities only
○ Face-to-face activities only
○ A combination of online and face-to-face activities
○ None of the above - this is not a priority for our school
○ Other (please explain)

7. Do adults associated with your school (e.g., parents or community members) volunteer time and effort to help promote and enrich your school community?

○ Yes
○ No

8. Please identify any adult-led groups or individuals that promote and enrich your school community.

- ☐ Parent Teacher Association (PTA)
- ☐ Parent Fundraising Events
- ☐ Parents involved in Virtual of F2F Field Trips
- ☐ Parents or Community Members as Guest Speakers
- ☐ Web Meetings (please explain)____
- ☐ Face-to-Face Events (please explain)____
- ☐ Click to write Choice____

9. Does your school provide online students with any kind of programming or support relating to community-building or social-emotional development?

- ◯ Yes
- ◯ No
- ◯ Unsure

10. Are you or your program planning to develop such non-academic support or experiences for online students in the future?

- ◯ Yes
- ◯ No
- ◯ Unsure

11. Please use the checklist below to indicate the types of physical, social, or non-academic program supports you or your program provide to students (select all that apply):

	Online Only	Face-to-Face Only	Both Online and Face-to-Face	Not Applicable
Social Gatherings	◯ Click to write Column 1 - Online Only - Social Gatherings	◯ Click to write Column 1 - Face-to-Face Only - Social Gatherings	◯ Click to write Column 1 - Both Online and Face-to-Face - Social Gatherings	◯ Click to write Column 1 - Not Applicable - Social Gatherings
Field Trips	◯ Click to write Column 1 - Online Only - Field Trips	◯ Click to write Column 1 - Face-to-Face Only - Field Trips	◯ Click to write Column 1 - Both Online and Face-to-Face - Field Trips	◯ Click to write Column 1 - Not Applicable - Field Trips
Recreationa	◯ Click	◯ Click	◯ Click to	◯ Click

8. Please identify any adult-led groups or individuals that promote and enrich your school community.

- ☐ Parent Teacher Association (PTA)
- ☐ Parent Fundraising Events
- ☐ Parents involved in Virtual of F2F Field Trips
- ☐ Parents or Community Members as Guest Speakers
- ☐ Web Meetings (please explain) ☐
- ☐ Face-to-Face Events (please explain) ☐
- ☐ Click to write Choice_____

9. Does your school provide online students with any kind of programming or support relating to community-building or social-emotional development?

- ◯ Yes
- ◯ No
- ◯ Unsure

10. Are you or your program planning to develop such non-academic support or experiences for online students in the future?

- ◯ Yes
- ◯ No
- ◯ Unsure

11. Please use the checklist below to indicate the types of physical, social, or non-academic program supports you or your program provide to students (select all that apply):

	Online Only	Face-to-Face Only	Both Online and Face-to-Face	Not Applicable
Social Gatherings	◯ Click to write Column 1 - Online Only - Social Gatherings	◯ Click to write Column 1 - Face-to-Face Only - Social Gatherings	◯ Click to write Column 1 - Both Online and Face-to-Face - Social Gatherings	◯ Click to write Column 1 - Not Applicable - Social Gatherings
Field Trips	◯ Click to write Column 1 - Online Only - Field Trips	◯ Click to write Column 1 - Face-to-Face Only - Field Trips	◯ Click to write Column 1 - Both Online and Face-to-Face - Field Trips	◯ Click to write Column 1 - Not Applicable - Field Trips

	Online Only	Face-to-Face Only	Both Online and Face-to-Face	Not Applicable
Recreational Events	◯ Click to write Column 1 - Online Only - Recreational Events	◯ Click to write Column 1 - Face-to-Face Only - Recreational Events	◯ Click to write Column 1 - Both Online and Face-to-Face - Recreational Events	◯ Click to write Column 1 - Not Applicable - Recreational Events
Exercise	◯ Click to write Column 1 - Online Only - Exercise	◯ Click to write Column 1 - Face-to-Face Only - Exercise	◯ Click to write Column 1 - Both Online and Face-to-Face - Exercise	◯ Click to write Column 1 - Not Applicable - Exercise
Showcases of Student Work	◯ Click to write Column 1 - Online Only - Showcases of Student Work	◯ Click to write Column 1 - Face-to-Face Only - Showcases of Student Work	◯ Click to write Column 1 - Both Online and Face-to-Face - Showcases of Student Work	◯ Click to write Column 1 - Not Applicable - Showcases of Student Work
Cultural Enrichment	◯ Click to write Column 1 - Online Only - Cultural Enrichment	◯ Click to write Column 1 - Face-to-Face Only - Cultural Enrichment	◯ Click to write Column 1 - Both Online and Face-to-Face - Cultural Enrichment	◯ Click to write Column 1 - Not Applicable - Cultural Enrichment
Service Projects	◯ Click to write Column 1 - Online Only - Service Projects	◯ Click to write Column 1 - Face-to-Face Only - Service Projects	◯ Click to write Column 1 - Both Online and Face-to-Face - Service Projects	◯ Click to write Column 1 - Not Applicable - Service Projects
Dances	◯ Click to write Column 1 - Online Only - Dances	◯ Click to write Column 1 - Face-to-Face Only - Dances	◯ Click to write Column 1 - Both Online and Face-to-Face - Dances	◯ Click to write Column 1 - Not Applicable - Dances

	Online Only	Face-to-Face Only	Both Online and Face-to-Face	Not Applicable
End of Year Celebration	◯	◯	◯	◯
Holiday Events (religious)	◯	◯	◯	◯
Holiday Events (non-sectarian)	◯	◯	◯	◯
Orientation Events	◯	◯	◯	◯
Clubs	◯	◯	◯	◯

	Online Only	Face-to-Face Only	Both Online and Face-to-Face	Not Applicable
Special Interest Groups	◯ Click to write Column 1 - Online Only - Special Interest Groups	◯ Click to write Column 1 - Face-to-Face Only - Special Interest Groups	◯ Click to write Column 1 - Both Online and Face-to-Face - Special Interest Groups	◯ Click to write Column 1 - Not Applicable - Special Interest Groups
Other (please explain)	◯ Click to write Column 1 - Online Only - Other (please explain)	◯ Click to write Column 1 - Face-to-Face Only - Other (please explain)	◯ Click to write Column 1 - Both Online and Face-to-Face - Other (please explain)	◯ Click to write Column 1 - Not Applicable - Other (please explain)

11. Of those events you selected, which ones seem to be the most popular in terms of participation?

12. Please describe any non-academic programs offered by you or your program that you feel are beneficial in terms of promoting social skills or building community among your online students.

13. How do K-12 students respond to social or recreational events hosted as a face-to-face supplement to a fully online academic program?

14. Would you be willing to be contacted so we can follow up and learn more about ways you or your institution supports holistic needs of K-12 online learners?

◯ Yes, I'll be happy to share ideas and approaches

◯ No, I'd rather not be contacted

◯ The following person specializes in this type of student support. Please see if s/he is able to discuss this further

15. Thanks for your willingness to share ideas and approaches for meeting non-academic needs of online learners. Please provide your preferred contact information here:

The Future of mLearning Begins with a Baseline Pedagogy
Elizabeth Cook[A]

Although the proliferation of mobile devices sets the stage for a revolution of education in developing countries and the evolution of education in developed countries, the formation of an effective mLearning pedagogy remains a bit elusive. The process of discovery outlined in this study begins with identifying and applying an appropriate learning theory to mobile learning, and by evaluating the role of technology in the classroom. The mLearning pedagogy advanced here is no different than others in its focus on content, instructional assets, cognitive processes and evaluations. However, with two parts harnessing the power of the Internet and the other two parts pushing technology to the background the result is a convergence of vital human interaction with nearly worldwide reach. A learning management system-less (LMS-less) approach is the element missing from previous studies and it is also the element that puts the immediate application of the mLearning pedagogy within reach.

Keywords: *elearning, mlearning, pedagogy, social constructivist theory, learning management system*

Introduction

Development of an effective mLearning pedagogy remains a bit elusive. mLearning is a term that refers to using mobile devices to learn (Valk, Rashid, & Elder, 2010). It differs from eLearning, which uses desktop and laptop computers to learn (Fisher & Baird, 2006), and from traditional learning, which is organized around an instructor in a physical classroom. Undeniably, advances in mobile technologies have improved student access to higher education (Valk et al., 2010), but integrating that same technology into the classroom design as an effective learning tool is much more challenging. It is important to differentiate between the role of mobile technology as a system for accessing the classroom and the role of mobile technology

---

[A] **Elizabeth Cook** is an Immigration Services Officer for US Citizenship and Immigration Services. Previously, she worked as a full-time Assistant Professor in the Department of International Relations, School of Security and Global Studies for the American Public University System. She taught several international relations courses including International Development. She has previous federal service with the Department of Defense and she is a veteran. She is currently a Ph.D. student at Walden University in the Public Policy and Administration program with a concentration in Homeland Security Policy and Coordination. She has completed the coursework and is currently writing her dissertation on the determinants behind child sex trafficking in Los Angeles County, California. She received her MS in International Relations from Troy University in 2007. She received her BS from Thomas Edison State College in Human Services and the Arnold Fletcher Award for exceptional achievement in independent learning in 2001. She is a member of the Pi Alpha Alpha and Golden Key International Honour Societies.

doi: 10.18278/il.4.2.4

in learning. Based on the interplay of existing learning management systems (LMSs) and mobile devices, new technological hurdles exist to extend access to both current eLearning students wishing to utilize mobile devices and to purely mLearning students that don't possess computers. Presumably, adjustments in the design by LMS developers and future advances in mobile technology will eventually resolve these issues. Until then, an LMS-less approach alleviates the need to force eLearning to fit mLearning and it promotes the development of a newly conceived mLearning classroom. An LMS-less approach also opens up more innate options for use in the pedagogy than are currently available to instructors in traditional or eLearning classrooms. With current access issues resolved through an LMS-less approach, the purpose of this study is to identify a pedagogical model for mLearning that works across mobile devices, but with a special focus on smartphones since they require the greatest departure from the current eLearning paradigm.

Literature Review

The pedagogical model begins with identifying an appropriate learning theory. As the name implies, learning theories are strategies to promote learning which, according to Gagne (1985) are defined as "change[s] in a learner's disposition and capabilities that can be reflected in behavior" (Wang, 2012, p. 10). These theories are often categorized based on common features, but they share the same overarching goal of guiding an instructor's pedagogy (Wang, 2012) hence, learning theories, are necessary precursors to developing pedagogy. Instructors should take note of their own role, the learner's role, and the relationship between the two (Wang, 2012) so that they can select the role that best fits student demographics and instructional topics. Therefore, two learning theories that support these roles are considered in this study: *social constructivism* and *connectivism*.

Social constructivism is a theory that is often associated with eLearning and connectivism is being debated as a learning theory underpinning mLearning (Anderson & Dron, 2011). However, connectivism hasn't developed enough to stand alone as a learning theory (Kop & Hill, 2008) in part because it seemingly overlooks the role of foundational learning on a topic before networking can be used to create new learning (Anderson & Dron, 2011). Social constructivism, which stems from Vygotsky and Dewey, builds upon the premise that foundational knowledge is a basic part of the construction of new knowledge (Anderson & Dron, 2011). Given the evolutionary nature of theories (Anderson & Dron, 2011; Baker-Eveleth, Chung, Eveleth, & O'Neill, 2011), a better way forward is to append a networking component into social constructivism until connectivism is either better developed or replaced by a new emerging theory. As a result, the learning theory being utilized in this study is social constructivism as derived from its cognitive-behaviorist roots (Anderson & Dron, 2011; Baker-Eveleth et al., 2011) with networking components borrowed from connectivism (Anderson & Dron, 2011). Broadly, the resulting pedagogy is content and asset driven with social activities and the opportunity to network included.

Drawing on the social constructivism theoretical framework, this study proceeds with sections on how social constructivism applies to mLearning, the specific role of technology in mLearning, the identification of a baseline mLearning pedagogy and conclusions. In short, mLearning has the potential to revolutionize learning in developing states and evolve learning in developed states through a convergence of the strengths related to the traditional and eLearning classrooms: human interaction and nearly world-wide reach. The LMS-less approach makes it relevant to today rather than at some unknown point in the future and the baseline pedagogy spans across academic disciplines. However, with so many innate options available for use in the baseline pedagogy, testing is needed to narrow them down for specific academic disciplines.

Applying Social Constructivism to mLearning

Anderson and Dron (2011) identify social constructivism as the second generation of distance learning education and connectivism as the third generation. Advocates of connectivism, Siemens and Downes advance the argument that "learning *is the process of* building networks of information, contacts and resources that are applied to real problems" (emphasis added) (Anderson & Dron, 2011, p. 87). Information, so the theory goes, is found and applied when and how it is needed (Anderson & Dron, 2011). This fits with "just-in-time" learning (Cruz-Flores & López-Morteo, 2010), but it overlooks the importance of having a foundational level of knowledge on a topic first. It is more reasonable to say that *once a foundation of learning on the topic has been achieved* "building networks of information, contacts and resources that are applied to real problems" results in new learning (Anderson & Dron, 2011, p. 87).

> **The supporting mobile technologies already exist in an LMS-less mLearning classroom, but the theory and resulting pedagogy hasn't evolved to take advantage of the opportunities at hand.**

For example, a learner with very little understanding of physics could go through the process of "building networks of information, contacts and resources that are applied to real problems" (Anderson & Dron, 2011, p. 87) without ever gaining a foundational level of understanding of physics. The ability to apply the information, which is contingent upon having a base level of understanding of it, is one link that is overlooked in connectivist theory. However, once that is achieved, the sources of information, contacts made and resources used (Anderson & Dron, 2011) that are associated to what is learned are kept by the learner, facilitated by technology, for future use and application, which should result in further learning. Networks create an opportunity for new learning, but connectivism is better described as a learning tool or asset that is best applied once foundational learning has been achieved. However, the notion that students create "networks of information, contacts and resources" for future use, at least in part through social interactions (Anderson & Dron, 2011, p. 87), is appealing and should be subsumed into social constructivism until connectivism is better developed or replaced.

Specifically as it relates to distance education, social constructivist theory evolved in tandem with advances in technology (Anderson & Dron, 2011). As one-to-one communication evolved into one-to-many and then many-to-many, social constructivism found its place in the distance learning classroom (Anderson & Dron, 2011). Arguably, social constructivism in this respect could only evolve *and* appear in practice as fast as the supporting technologies allowed. Today, the opposite is true. The supporting mobile technologies already exist in an LMS-less mLearning classroom, but the theory and resulting pedagogy hasn't evolved to take advantage of the opportunities at hand. Chief among them is better meeting the expectations of the net generation of students.

The net generation, the first generation to always have the Internet, is substantially different than past generations of students that studied for tests and whose knowledge was based on instructor-centered modes for transferring information like lectures and handouts and the resources contained in local libraries (Fisher & Baird, 2006). The net generation seeks to learn on the spot, "just-in-time and just-in-place"(Cruz-Flores & López-Morteo, 2010, p. 10) as the need for the information develops and mLearning enables that paradigm shift (Fisher & Baird, 2006). Social constructivist theory applied to an mLearning classroom environment and corresponding pedagogy must account for the learning needs and social expectations of the net generation by wholly embracing a socially based student-centered pedagogy (Anderson & Dron, 2011; Fisher & Baird, 2006). As such, the application of technology in the pedagogy must allow students to "communicate, negotiate, socialize and learn" and, thereby network, while "on-the-go" (Cruz-Flores & López-Morteo, 2010, p. 9).

The Role of Technology in mLearning

Identifying how students access knowledge and the basic focal point of instructor interaction as it exists today determines the role of technology in learning. For example, in a traditional classroom it is very difficult to wholly deviate from an instructor centered delivery of knowledge and a content-driven approach since it is expected that students will access knowledge through the instructor. Social activities in that classroom environment may include informal student presentations or brainstorming sessions. In an eLearning environment, access to knowledge isn't centered on the instructor or the student, but rather on the LMS being used, the technology that underpins it and the classroom design (Anderson & Dron, 2011). Students independently access and review the course materials prior to engaging in socially oriented activities like those on a discussion board.

Obviously, technology has always played an important role in distance education (Fisher & Baird, 2006). In the eLearning environment, students work from a desktop centered application on a traditional or laptop computer (Fisher & Baird, 2006). However, that won't work well in the mLearning environment especially on smartphones because screen sizes are much smaller (Fisher & Baird, 2006; Valk et al., 2010) and battery life and memory are limited (Fisher & Baird, 2006). A smaller screen size on any device means that a text-based transfer of data is cumbersome for the student (Fisher & Baird, 2006). As a result, mLearning must substantially deviate from the eLearning paradigm and leverage the strengths associated to small, hand-held mobile devices toward creating new learning in students. In short, the content should be geared toward specific devices (Fisher & Baird, 2006) and around the interplay of instructors/students, data/technology, and time control/session work integrity (Cruz-Flores & López-Morteo, 2010) by integrating the "human-to-human" and "human-to-computer" aspects (Lambropoulos, Faulkner, & Culwin, 2012, p. 297). Practically speaking these can take the form of real-time chats, screen sharing, team rather than individual interactions, and formats that showcase participation (Cruz-Flores & López-Morteo, 2010).

With the device specifications and social constructivist theory in mind, the course design should be socially based. It should account for data transmission and socially-based dialog between the course participants (Lambropoulos et al., 2012). The social presence of the participants (Aragon, 2003) and the social interaction of students with the instructor (Baker-Eveleth et al., 2011) are crucial to promoting a social learning environment or community. This social interaction can take shape in the form of mentoring sessions, practice sessions and debriefing sessions (Baker-Eveleth et al., 2011). The course design should provide opportunities for students to observe, imitate and model behavior as a part of the learning environment (Baker-Eveleth et al., 2011). Students should experience meaning and feel like they belong to the group, which in turn should become a part of their identity and result in increased involvement (Baker-Eveleth et al., 2011).

A critique of the technology used for eLearning revolves around its use to disseminate information and organize the classroom environment through an LMS rather than on creating learning in students (Lambropoulos et al., 2012). Meaningful discussions, a crucial component of a successful pedagogy based on social constructivist theory, are difficult to orchestrate in an eLearning environment (Lambropoulos et al., 2012) due to the limitations in the technology associated to the LMS. Social awareness, which includes both presence and copresence, is needed in an eLearning environment, but current LMS' provide a weak platform for students to observe themselves individually and in relation to other students (Lambropoulos et al., 2012). These weaknesses are demonstrated by nonparticipation, passive participation (reading only) and low participation in discussions (Lambropoulos et al., 2012). Two ideas studied by Lambropoulos, Faulkner and Culwin (2012) to improve both the quantity and quality of posts by students are to add visualizations regarding individual participation and participation relative to the rest of the group (e.g. who is at the center of the conversation) and to create a Collaborative eLearning Episode (CeLE) by having students use drop-down lists to label the content of a post (e.g. suggestion, question, agreement, etc.). This information, which showed the most promise in their study, can be used to show students what they contribute to class discussions along with their strengths and weaknesses (Lambropoulos et al., 2012).

The technology used for mLearning is a bit different. Smartphones and other mobile devices are used to gain access to the class and for new learning. Smartphones differ from traditional phones due to their data (Valk et al., 2010) and video features. Practically speaking, that means that students can use their phones to upload/download files like .pdfs and Word documents from online libraries. They can also watch videos either provided by the instructor or that already exist on the Internet like those on YouTube.

It is widely accepted that eLearning via desktop and laptop computer increases student access to education and LMS-less mLearning via smartphones and other mobile devices increases that access even more (Valk et al., 2010). Without the need to purchase a computer and separate Internet service, mLearning based on devices and services the student already possesses is less expensive and users are already familiar with them (Valk et al., 2010). They are expected to transform the student experience into one that is customizable and individual in ways that promote both situated and authentic learning (Valk et al., 2010). The ability to provide not just timely, but nearly continual feedback also promotes student learning and reflection (Valk et al., 2010).

LMS-less mLearning provides the opportunity to push the technology from the forefront of the class like in is in eLearning to the background. It allows instructors and students to connect and engage "just-in-time and just-in-place" (Cruz-Flores & López-Morteo, 2010), in ways that make the underlying technology largely invisible. This helps keep the orientation of the classroom design on the learning theory and pedagogy rather than on the technology. Technology provides options for the application of the learning theory in the pedagogy, which is described by Anderson and Dron (2011) as a "hardening" of the pedagogy (p. 81). Undeniably, those options are rightly taken into consideration in the pedagogy (Anderson & Dron, 2011), but technology shouldn't dictate it. Perhaps the best way to describe it is that the technology should be so invisible to the student that it is taken for granted. An eLearning student today might describe the eLearning classroom as being computer based or online. The goal of mLearning should be to have students describe it as person-to-person with adding that contact is facilitated through smartphones or other mobile technology only as an afterthought.

If the real estate mantra is "location, location, location" then the mLearning mantra for LMS-less classrooms is "options, options, options". There are so many options on how an instructor can leverage technology in an LMS-less mLearning classroom to create new learning that it is nearly overwhelming. For example, at least 16 well-known options exist for students to read an ebook associated to an mLearning classroom. A few of the most popular reader apps are Kindle, Nook and Google Play Books. Google Play Books is probably the most universal since it isn't tied to a device like a Kindle or a Nook. To use this technology in an mLearning classroom, an instructor only needs to ensure that the course text(s) are available on multiple apps. The student chooses which one to use.

A Conceptual Baseline Pedagogy for mLearning

Anderson and Dron (2011) explain three generations of distance learning pedagogies as a "dance" between technology and pedagogy (p. 81). Although theory is well-represented in the article, it is strangely absent from this dance. Imagine instead a dance between theory and pedagogy where technology cuts in. Theory provides strategic direction, whereby pedagogy applies those ideas and technology provides options for access and learning.

How students access knowledge determines the classroom type. For example, traditional learning, eLearning, mLearning and hybrid classes are types of learning whereby knowledge is accessed in a more formal, facilitated setting. They are different than a library, which is also an access point for knowledge, but it isn't a formal one-- meaning that the transfer of knowledge isn't facilitated by an instructor. Identifying *how* students will access the classroom environment is important because it impacts the application of the learning theory in the pedagogy (please see *Figure 1*).

A pedagogy includes the presentation of content, instructional assets, cognitive processes for the student, and evaluation of the learning achieved (Nish, n.d.). mLearning pedagogy is no different. Pedagogies associated to traditional classrooms are content-driven and instructor-centered (Anderson & Dron, 2011) and pedagogies associated to eLearning classrooms are LMS-driven and instructor-guided (Anderson & Dron, 2011). In an mLearning classroom, the pedagogy is Internet-driven and socially-centered. Content is identified by the instructor and available to the student

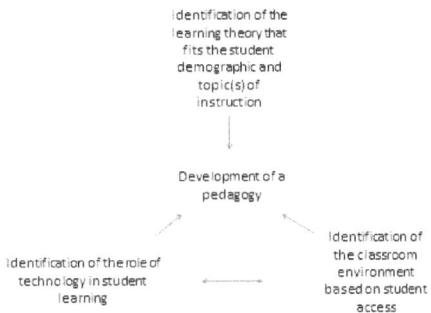

Figure 1. Interactions between theory, pedagogy, and technology

through the Internet. Presentation of the content depends on its form. Live, written, audio and audio/video are all options. The instructional assets related to learning are also related to, and provided by the Internet. Cognitive processes can vary based on the topic and student demographics due to the flexibility provided by the Internet and evaluations can include old techniques like quizzes and papers and new techniques like the "just-in-place" (Cruz-Flores & López-Morteo, 2010) application of new skills. Expressed in a formula an mLearning pedagogy looks like this: *social constructivist theory (networking component) + Internet content + Internet assets + instructor-to-student/student-to-student cognitive processes + instructor-to-student/student-to-student evaluations = a baseline mLearning pedagogy.* Leveraging the means and instruments available through the Internet to deliver course content and the instructional assets provides more natural options to "harden" the pedagogy (Anderson & Dron, 2011, p. 81) than are typically employed in traditional and eLearning classrooms. Although the cognitive processes and evaluations also use the Internet, the technology is pushed to the

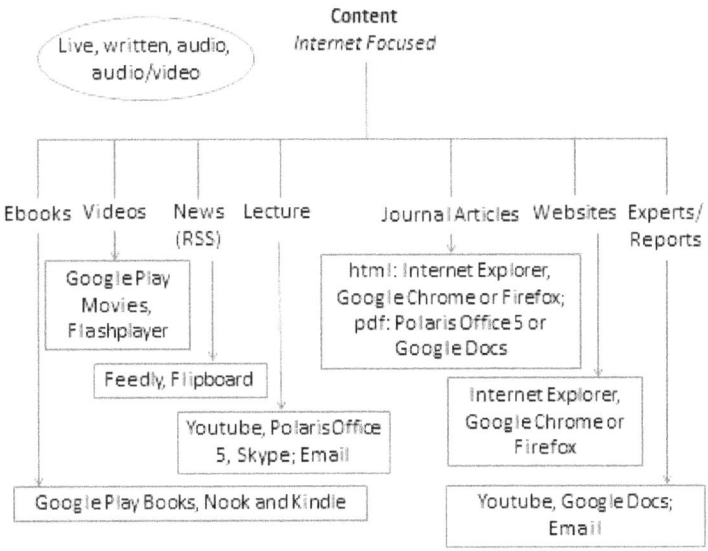

Figure 2. Examples related to the content portion of the pedagogy.

Internet Learning

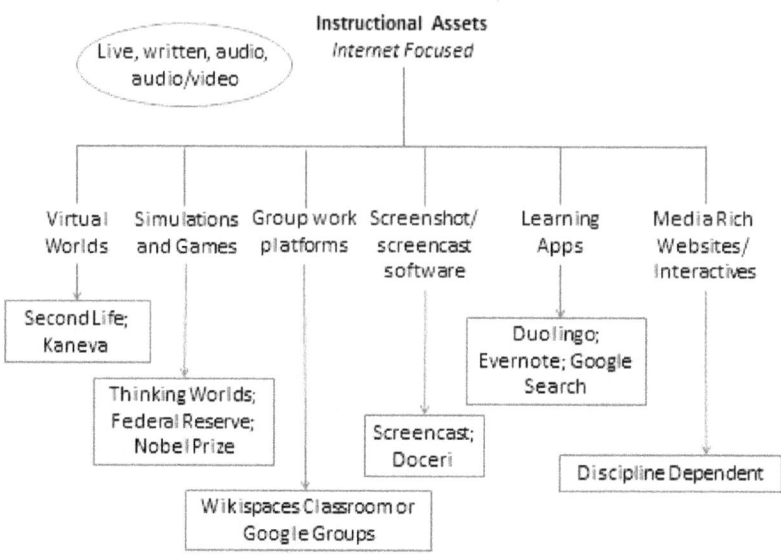

Figure 3. Examples related to the instructional assets portion of the pedagogy.

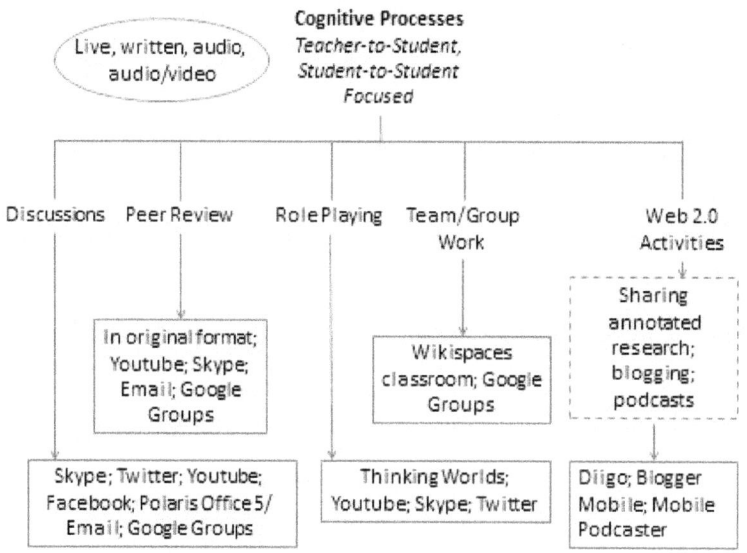

Figure 4. Examples related to the cognitive processes portion of the pedagogy.

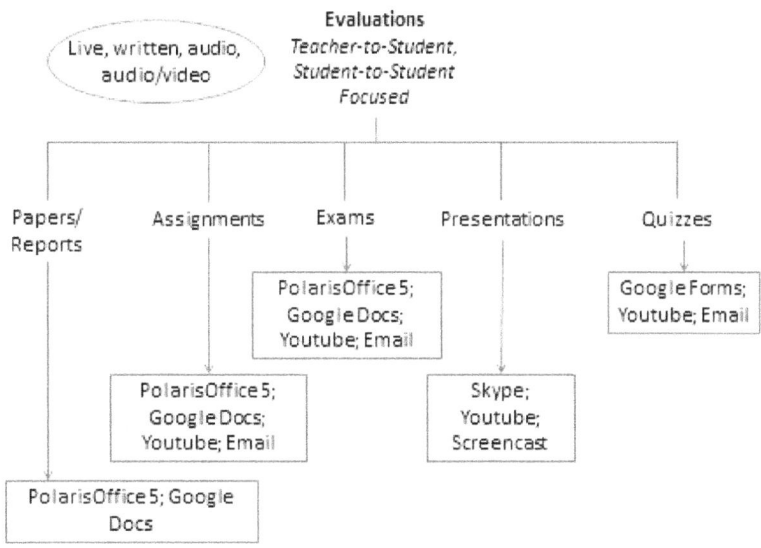

Figure 5. Examples related to the evaluations portion of the pedagogy.

background. The focus in those two areas of the pedagogy is on instructor-to-student and student-to-student interaction. To better express this baseline mLearning pedagogy, the following figures identify a few of the options related to each of the four core areas of the pedagogy:

Certainly, this pedagogy is familiar and many of these options are currently in use in traditional or eLearning classrooms. The point here is to draw in the strengths of those pedagogies while further developing the role of technology for access and creating new learning. Again, the LMS-less approach takes advantage of market demand for compatibility, which makes mLearning wholly available today.

Strengths of the mLearning Pedagogy

There are a few things that are easier or more convenient to do on a mobile device, like a smartphone, than they are on a laptop or desktop computer. For example, microblogging similar to Twitter could occur spontaneously rather than in a formal study session. Microblogging could be used in a number of ways in the classroom. For example, students could use microblogging to report, converse, and archive items (Anderson & Dron, 2011), such as sources related to a particular topic, brainstorm, vote on a debate or topic, or provide a running commentary like at the bottom of a news channel. Most of these should not serve as independent cognitive processes or evaluations, but they can be useful tools in the classroom. Microblogging, in particular, helps close the gap between the life of the student outside and inside the classroom because participation is not limited to formal class or study times. Also, providing a running commentary of an event helps close the gap between the theoretical and the applied. For example, a student could attend a local political speech or even watch a documentary on something like the Rwandan genocide and tweet about it throughout, which could form the basis of a more formal and reflective cognitive process on that topic. Imagine forum discussions supplemented each week by student reporting and impressions of events, documentaries and the like. There exists a whole new level of dynamism that would be hard to match with a laptop or desktop computer. Being less formal, it also adds to the social interaction among students as they respond to tweets about the topic and otherwise network with each other. This idea also works in reverse, meaning that the instructor can tweet on an upcoming topic as the resident expert, which would improve the teaching, social and cognitive presence of the instructor all at once. Microblogging can add an element of continual discourse, however brief, outside of formally submitted and graded evaluations that are currently sparse in traditional or eLearning environments.

Another major benefit of mobile learning is that it can occur in very small increments. Students can leverage short expanses of down time like an unexpected wait at a doctor's office to learn. Given that mobile devices are often carried for other reasons, prior planning isn't required. Students can decide spontaneously to learn because the mood struck or opportunity knocked. Mobile learning should result in increases in new learning as students increase the total amount of time spent on learning and learning activities like thinking and analysis because they are no longer tethered to a formal class or study space and time.

Keeping social constructivist theory with a networking component in mind, cognitive processes can take a number of forms. For example, using a flipped approach, students are able review the course materials and submit questions or topics for discussion, which the instructor can choose from based on the course objectives for that week (University of Washington, 2015). Drawing from the technological options available to "harden" the pedagogy (Anderson & Dron, 2011, p. 81), the course materials could include written, audio or audio video components that are instructor-generated, or from materials developed by experts in the field that already exist on the Internet. The proposed questions or topics can be submitted by tweets on Twitter, and the discussion can be held synchronously via Skype, or asynchronously via Facebook or YouTube. In another flipped example, students can review the course materials and take a quiz early in the week with weaknesses forming the basis of the next discussion (Smith, 2013). Technologically, the quiz can be administered via Google Forms in a written format or with the questions provided by the instructor in a YouTube video. In this particular instance, students could provide their answers by emailing the link to a locked YouTube video back to the instructor. Another option is to administer the quiz via YouTube, but have the students provide their answers using Polaris Office 5 or Google Docs via email. Still another option is to email students a word document with the question and have them use Polaris Office 5 or Google Docs to edit the document to include their answers and email it back. More options exist that can be selected as required.

Imagine hands-on projects captured by video or group projects supported by six or more underlying means of communication for research, coordination, application and submission. In short, the strength of the baseline mLearning pedagogy is in its ability to be individually tailored to particular disciplines and pedagogical needs. Unlike the traditional classroom that isn't well set up to leverage the Internet to its fullest potential and the eLearning LMS that is limited by its underlying technology, the limitation factors here are related to the ability of the instructor to envision the possibilities.

Weaknesses of the mLearning Pedagogy

Despite the pedagogy's strengths, there also exist some weaknesses. First, since an LMS-less mLearning classroom isn't a place students go *to*, this type of learning environment could feel very abstract and unreal to students, which would presumably negatively affect their ability to successfully stay connected with and complete courses. A simple webpage to post announcements and provide links to the course materials for that week could help alleviate this until students adapt to the environment. Also, students could receive announcements via an RSS feed if available. Second, regulatory controls could be difficult given the number of options available. Third, abiding by laws like Family Educational Rights and Privacy Act (FERPA) may not be readily achievable in an LMS-less classroom (Mastors, 2013). Finally, a virtual campus for registration, etc. is still required, so some form of software overhead is needed.

Conclusion

mLearning has the potential to create a revolution of learning in developing countries and an evolution of learning in developed countries through a convergence of: 1) human interaction - a strength in a traditional classroom; and, 2), nearly world-wide reach - a strength of an eLearning classroom. The revolutionary potential in developing countries comes from the ability to provide education to people living in the global south *at a level never before experienced*. Six billion people in the world have mobile phones (UN News Centre, 2013) and 2.1 billion people have broadband subscriptions for them (mobiThinking, 2014). Of those, 1.16 billion are located in the global south (mobiThinking, 2014). The evolutionary potential in developed countries comes from the ability to expand mLearning so that it incorporates other mobile devices and fee based apps, which could provide a more cohesive learning experience for students.

In both environments, pedagogies related to mLearning should be driven by theory and envisioned without the dependence of an LMS in order to take advantage of the demand for compatibility between devices in the civilian market. Two portions of the pedagogy, content/presentation and instructional assets, should leverage the options available on the Internet. Doing so provides more options for use in the pedagogy than are currently available to instructors in traditional or eLearning classrooms. The remaining two portions of the pedagogy, cognitive processes and evaluations, should focus on instructor-to-student and student-to-student interaction by pushing the technology to the background.

Significant testing across disciplines is needed to identify the best practices. Having a nearly unlimited number of options is great providing that cognitive processes are organized, scaffolded and result in new learning. Presumably, the options that create new learning in natural sciences aren't necessarily the same options that create new learning in other fields like history. Likewise, the options that best fit one culture won't necessarily be the same ones that best fit another culture particularly considering the differences between developing and developed countries.

References

Anderson, T., & Dron, J. (2011). Three Generations of Distance Education Pedagogy. *International Review of Research in Open and Distance Learning, 12*(3), 80–97.

Aragon, S. (2003). Creating Social Presence in Online Environments. *New Directions for Adult and Continuing Education, 100*, 57–68.

Baker-Eveleth, L., Chung, Y., Eveleth, D., & O'Neill, M. (2011). Developing A Community Of Practice Through Learning Climate, Leader Support, And Leader Interaction. *American Journal of Business Education, 4*(2), 33–40.

Cruz-Flores, R., & López-Morteo, G. (2010). A Framework for Educational Collaborative Activities Based on Mobile Devices A Support to the Instructional Design. *International Journal of Interactive Mobile Technologies, 4*(3), 9–18.

Fisher, M., & Baird, D. (2006). Making mLearning Work: Utilizing Mobile Technology for Active Exploration, Collaboration, Assessment, and Reflection in Higher Education. *J. Educational Technology Systems, 35*(1), 3–30.

Kop, R., & Hill, A. (2008). Connectivism: Learning theory of the future or vestige of the past? *International Review of Research in Open and Distance Learning, 9*(3), 1–13.

Lambropoulos, N., Faulkner, X., & Culwin, F. (2012). Supporting social awareness in collaborative elearning. *British Journal of Educational Technology, 43*(2), 295–306.

Mastors, E. (2013, October 17). Personal conversation via telephone.

mobiThinking. (2014, May 2). Global mobile statistics 2013 Part A: Mobile subscribers; handset market share; mobile operators. Retrieved May 20, 2013, from https://mobiforge.com/research-analysis/global-mobile-statistics-2014-part-b-mobile-web-mobile-broadband-penetration-3g4g-subscribers-and-ne

Nish, S. (n.d.). What is Pedagogy ? - YouTube. Retrieved October 23, 2013, from http://www.youtube.com/watch?v=jkoRR670fj8

Smith, S. (2013). The Data-Driven Classroom. Retrieved August 9, 2013, from http://americanradioworks.publicradio.org/features/tomorrows-college/keyboard-college/data-driven-classroom.html

University of Washington. (2015). Flipping the classroom. Retrieved from http://www.washington.edu/teaching/teaching-resources/engaging-students-in-learning/flipping-the-classroom/

UN News Centre. (2013, March 21). Deputy UN chief calls for urgent action to tackle global sanitation crisis. Retrieved from http://www.un.org/apps/news/story.asp?NewsID=44452#.VhBb_vlViko

Valk, J.-H., Rashid, A., & Elder, L. (2010). Using Mobile Phones to Improve Educational Outcomes: An Analysis of Evidence from Asia. *International Review of Research in Open and Distance Learning, 11*(1), 117–140.

Wang, V. (2012). Understanding and promoting learning theories. *International Forum of Teaching and Studies, 8*(2), 5–11.

Employee Motivations for Workplace Learning and the Role of Elearning in the Workplace

Jason G. Caudill[A]

Workplace learning is increasingly important in the dynamic competitive environment faced by organizations throughout the world. As the needs of a successful organization continually change there is a need for the employees of that organization, at every level, to update and expand their skills to match the needs of the organization. This places workplace learning in the position of serving employees at different levels of the organization and with different professional skills and responsibilities. In order to best ground workplace learning design as an aspect of the organization's overall strategy it is important to recognize the common elements of all workplace learning design and their importance in supporting the success of the firm. These common elements are increasingly best served by the use of workplace elearning approaches. This paper will examine workplace learning as a strategic focus of the modern firm and the common elements that are present across all types of training in the workplace as well as the unique elements of elearning in the workplace.

Keywords: *workplace learning, elearning, learning organization, ADDIE*

Introduction

The competitive environment for almost every industry is increasingly dynamic and both the work and technology environments are rapidly changing. Kyndt, Raes, Dochy, and Janssens (2012) explain that these changes and the shifting focus to knowledge work are driving firms to shift their focus to more highly skilled workers. These changes are challenging companies to continually update and improve their processes and, as a result, employees at every level are increasingly expected to continually learn new skills to keep pace with the changing needs of their company and their customers. While the content of learning activities differs among industries and even among different categories of employees in a single firm, there are many common themes that support the need for, and delivery of, workplace learning for employees.

By addressing these common elements, firms can better construct an overall philosophy of workplace learning for their employees. The process will be similar to many other strategic management

---

[A] **Dr. Jason Caudill** currently serves as an Associate Professor of Business at King University. His education includes a BS in Business Administration, an MBA, and a PhD in Instructional Technology from the University of Tennessee as well as a graduate certificate in Strategic Management from Harvard Extension School. His research interests include technology management, online learning, and the management and markets of higher education.

doi: 10.18278/il.4.2.5

processes, with the first steps focusing on identification of need and subsequent steps working to identify, implement, and evaluate the solutions to the identified need. Needs at the corporate level may need to be addressed at multiple employee levels, with multiple learning approaches, but the core of the process should be a unified strategy to improve employee and company performance to better serve the customer.

These employee needs and motivations apply across learning platforms, but the delivery mechanism for instruction in the workplace is increasingly that of elearning. In the context of the overall need for workplace learning and employee motivations for learning a well-designed elearning program addresses the needs of multiple stakeholders. To address this workplace learning as a whole is discussed and then the elearning component is added into the context of the broader workplace.

> Beyond the tools used to perform the job, employees today are also responsible for learning about changes to the company's approach to doing business, changes to what customers need, and changes to the competitive environment.

Learning's Role in the Workplace

Traditional views of functional areas in a firm may relegate workplace learning to only a human resource function. The reality of the modern environment, however, is quite different. Harmon (2015) identifies Learning & Growth Measures as one element of a departmental scorecard applied to departments, processes, and activities across an entire firm. This expansion of learning into every part of a firm is a natural extension of the need for all functional areas in a firm to continually grow and improve service to the increasingly complex and competitive external environment in which all industries are working today.

Learning activities in the modern firm can encompass a number of different areas. Technical learning involves developing new skills for new tools, whether those skills are applied to a new software application, new manufacturing equipment, or some other technical aspect of the business. This type of learning is often the first type considered because of the rapid advance of technology in all aspects of life but it is not the only area of change and learning for today's workers.

Beyond the tools used to perform the job, employees today are also responsible for learning about changes to the company's approach to doing business, changes to what customers need, and changes to the competitive environment. These learning activities ultimately connect to the overall corporate strategy of the firm and, by extension, impact every employee, in every department, at every level (see *Figure 1*).

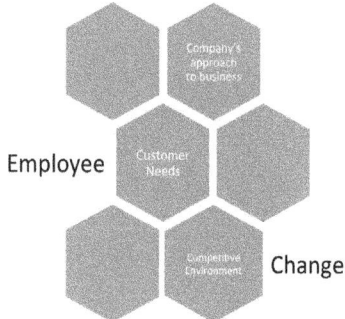

Figure 1. Employees are responsible for change according to customer needs.

Learning in the modern workplace is much more than a question of introductory training or policy updates, although those elements do require training to maintain employee knowledge and skills. Learning today defines the competitive firm as a whole; the market rewards learning organizations. Pantouvakis & Bouranta (2013) explain that, , "...the success of an organization does not depend solely on the current levels of employee skills, capabilities and knowledge, but mainly on their ability to improve themselves on an ongoing basis" (p 49).

Investments in employee learning have been shown to benefit organizations' innovative performance (Sung & Choi, 2014), positively contribute to knowledge transfer for multi-national corporations (Minbaeva, Pederson, Bjorkman, Fey, & Park, 2014), and is positively related to overall firm performance (Aragon, Jimenez, & Valle, 2014). Other studies identify other specific benefits to the firm of employee learning but clearly the firm as a whole is improved when employees are more knowledgeable. Given that the firm, as a whole, impacts a reasonable part of the workplace learning approach, and also includes identifying how common factors across the firm impact the design and administration of learning for employees.

Design Factors in Workplace Learning

The first step in approaching the design of a workplace learning program is to define what workplace learning is and what it is intended to accomplish. Wang (2011) defines workplace learning, "as the means, processes, and activities by which employees learn in the workplace from basic skills to high technology and management practice that are immediately applicable to workers' jobs, duties, and roles" (p 196). This definition aligns with the identified benefits of workplace learning as it addresses learning across an organization at different levels and in different specialties but all focused on improving the work of the firm.

While there are multiple approaches to learning design Simmons (2011) identifies the ADDIE model as a good match for workplace learning because, "...the model calls for continual evaluation, much like the strategic management, continuous improvement, and monitor and adjust/backwards design models commonly used in business" (p 3). This focus on continual improvement and monitoring is a good fit for the dynamic competitive environment in which modern firms are operating. With a focus on the core steps of the ADDIE model; Analysis, Design, Development, Implementation, and Evaluation, a firm can develop quality workplace learning opportunities for the workforce that will benefit overall organizational performance.

> "...the success of an organization does not depend solely on the current levels of employee skills, capabilities and knowledge, but mainly on their ability to improve themselves on an ongoing basis" (Pantouvakis & Bouranta, 2013, p 49).

The ADDIE model approach to learning design provides the flexibility to address needs at any level and in any department of a firm. In reviewing the approach, it closely mirrors many of the strategic management problem solving frameworks. Analysis provides an opportunity to look at current practices and current results and identify where there is a need for change. Design creates possible solutions to the identified need. Development identifies and builds a selected solution from the design phase. Implementation takes action to apply the selected solution to the

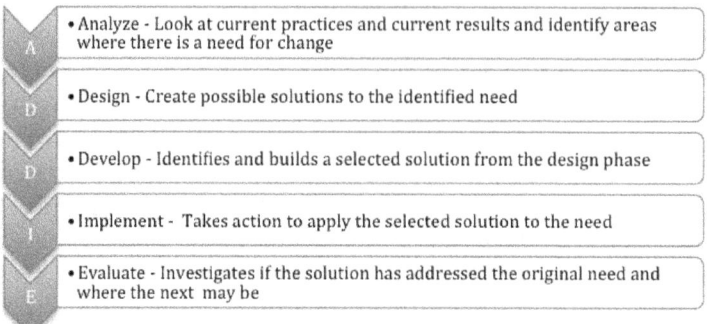

Figure 2. ADDIE Model Steps

need and evaluation completes the cycle by investigating if the solution has addressed the original need and where the next need may be (see *Figure 2*).

This overall model of learning development, and its similarity to the decision-making and management models used throughout the business world, highlights the extent to which workplace learning is truly a distributed activity. This distributed nature lends itself to viewing workplace learning as an overall organizational strategy rather than a compartmentalized activity for a specific department or a specific user group. To better understand this, the common elements of training for different groups in the organization will be explored.

Individual Participation in Workplace Learning

While workplace learning is an activity to benefit the organization as a whole, all of the learning ultimately takes place at the individual level. In order to effectively deliver a workplace learning experience the individual must be addressed. Kyndt & Baert (2013) explain the development of an individual's participation in a workplace learning experience as starting, "…from a generally formulated or felt need that evolves into an educational need, which leads toward an intention to participate in learning and a concrete educational demand, resulting in the actual participation in a learning activity" (p 275).

This first step in the individual learning experience matches the first step in the ADDIE model of workplace development; recognition of a need. For the individual this is an educational need. This recognition of need leads employees to engage in learning activities for a broad variety of reasons, including their ability to maintain performance and retain employment and also to learn how to operate in the increasingly dynamic work environments of today's organizations (Billet & Choi, 2013). Employees clearly recognize a need for learning in connection to their role in the workplace, but the next step is achieving the necessary motivation to take action to satisfy their perceived need.

Motivation for learning occurs on several different levels: the individual level, the learning activity level, and the social context level (Kyndt & Baert, 2013). While individual motivation is addressed here the role of the organization in serving the learning activity and the social context of the learning will be explored in the following section. McQuaid, Raeside, Canduela, Egdell, and Lindsay (2012) found that for low-skilled workers motivating factors for pursuing training included getting a better job, personal improvement, being better at work, and improving skills. These motivations for learning are reflected in Kyndt, Govaerts, Keunen, and Dochy's (2012) work that identifies learning intention as an employee's plan to remedy perceived needs in knowledge, skill, or attitudes necessary to perform their jobs. Knowledge workers, which encompass an ever-increasing number of the modern workforce, are shown to have similar learning motivations to low-skilled workers. Batalla-Busquets & Pacheco-Bernal (2013) identify learning motivations for skilled workers as including personal growth, belonging to the organization, and expected career progress.

These similar motivations across employee categories identifies that addressing concerns of professional advancement and personal growth are necessary to effectively deliver learning opportunities for an organization. The positive aspect of this is that employees recognize the need for continued learning opportunities and also identify the value that potentially comes from such activities. The challenge to the modern firm is to create an environment that successfully delivers that experience to the worker.

Organizational Involvement in Workplace Learning

Organizations, as the ultimate beneficiaries of workplace learning, have an important role in the overall learning environment and the motivation of employee learning. To retain the best employees, organizations in today's market must provide a positive climate for both work and learning (Govaerts, et al., 2010). Kyndt, Raes, et al. (2012) explain that for an organization it is, "…important to know how employees learn and which factors contribute to a stimulating learning environment" (p 272). This one statement speaks to two important roles of the firm in delivering workplace learning. The first is to provide proper motivation, through a supportive environment, and the second is to deliver a valuable learning product to the employee.

The core factor in providing motivation for employees to engage in learning activities is the design of the job itself. Kyndt, Govaerts, et al. (2012) identify five job characteristics that influence employee learning motivation:

- The degree of autonomy
- The content and complexity of the job
- The learning potential
- The task variety
- The mobility opportunities the job offers – p 183

Thus, at the very beginning of an organization's role in the workplace learning process the fundamentals of organizational behavior are in play. Job design plays a critical role in preparing employees for motivation and participation in workplace learning and includes such diverse ideas as organizational structure, job expansion, job rotation, and retention and promotion policies. This point should not be surprising. As organizations transition to being learning organizations and all employees are impacted by the demands for continuing learning it is natural that the fundamental design of the firm will be influenced by the changes occurring everywhere else. The first step in being effective in workplace learning is to design and operate a workplace that aligns with the modern structure of a learning organization.

Moving from job design to specific elements of organizational culture that can motivate employee learning there are three organizational learning environment factors: managerial support, job support, and organizational support (Cheng, Wang, Moormann, Olaniran, & Chen, 2012). This con-tinues the trend that has been identified in the construction of a learning organization. Support for workplace learning is not a single department or a single level within the organization; support to motivate employee learning happens across the organization and throughout the organizational chart. Everybody in the organization has a role to play in building a positive learning environment for employees (see *Figure 3*).

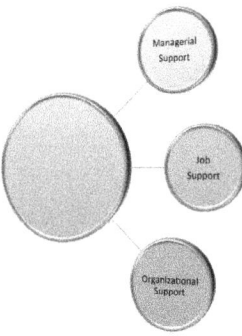

Figure 3. The three organizational learning environment factors: managerial support, job support, and organizational support.

This helps to frame the overall discussion of workplace learning and its importance to remaining competitive in the modern, dynamic market. While the engagement of the individual employee in learning activities may be the most visible element of workplace learning what is actually happening is that organizations are becoming learning organizations. As learning organizations, the effective use of employee learning leads to positive organizational performance and positive economic performance (Pantouvakis & Bouranta, 2013). The delivery phase of workplace learning will also encompass all areas of the firm.

Once an effective climate and support structure has been established, a company must then effectively deliver the learning experience in which employees have been motivated to engage. Kyndt, Raes, et al. (2012) explain the need for a new perspective on the delivery of learning as a whole:

> ...because of the rapidly changing context in which organizations operate, a necessity arises for employees to learn in a way that involves integrating materials from different sources, relating new information to prior knowledge, applying knowledge differentially according to the situation. In other words, a need for a deep approach to learning comes to the fore (p 272).

The delivery of the learning experience for employees most directly involves the implementation and evaluation stages of the ADDIE model, although the earlier analysis, design, and development stages directly impact the success of the program. As with the individual employees, firms first must recognize the need for learning to take place. This recognition of need can be either an emphasis on repairing an identified failing in the firm or it can be a process of finding and enhancing existing solutions to make further improvements to a process (Govaerts, et al., 2010). Once the need is identified then the design and development phases can be pursued.

Designing and developing a learning experience for employees, regardless of the topic of the instruction or the role of the employee, is perhaps the most important unseen activity involved in the delivery of workplace learning. At this stage specific goals are identified for the training and details such as delivery format, scheduling, and instructors are selected. While employees do want to engage in learning when there is a perceived need and a motivating atmosphere, they need to have identifiable goals for the experience in order to fully engage (Kyndt, Govaerts, et al., 2012). Once the goal is set and the employee engages with the training proper development helps to ensure that the employee remains engaged and successfully completes the learning process that will improve employee and firm performance.

Individuals engaging in workplace learning are motivated by factors such as personal improvement and career advancement. This means that they have an expectation that the learning experience will help them to achieve positive, meaningful outcomes. What this means to the development process is that the material that is covered, and the way it is delivered, must be relevant to the individuals who are participating. This means aligning content and delivery with the participants' responsibilities and the way that the firm conducts their operations. By properly grounding the delivery as a useful, applicable model the participants will have the opportunity to see a linkage between their learning and their work. With these development tasks complete the company can move to the visible part of the ADDIE process, the delivery.

Much of the delivery of the learning experience will be defined in the development stage. Delivery itself will mean deploying the planned learning process to identified participants to address the identified need. If the learning experience is well designed and well developed then the execution of the plan should go well. It is at this point that employees have the opportunity to directly engage with the content and begin the process of absorbing the material and learning how the new information or skills can improve their work. At this point in the process the visible activity of the learning event concludes for participants, but for the firm the delivery precedes the final stage of evaluation.

As with any strategic initiative workplace learning needs to generate a positive return for the firm. This means that learning that occurs needs to be properly and consistently applied when individual participants return to their jobs. Determining whether or not this takes place, and whether or not the modified behavior has the desired impact on company performance, is the role of evaluation.

The evaluation following a workplace learning event may take multiple forms. In examining changes to quality metrics, production output, or other quantitative measures the evaluation is relatively simple. Over time following the training the quantitative data can be tracked, trends and performance benchmarks can be established, and correlations can be identified regarding whether training did or did not have a positive impact on employee performance. These quantitative measures, however, are only indicators of the learning's outcome and do not entirely address the efficacy of the program.

The ideal outcome of a workplace learning exercise is to positively impact the culture of the organization. While such a chance may manifest in quantitative outcomes, the real value of the change is one of moving towards a high performing culture. This means that employees adopt new ways of doing things and also integrate new ways of thinking and new attitudes in relation to their work. These kinds of changes in relation to workplace learning experiences help to move the firm to a true learning organization. The net effect of such cultural shifts in an organization is part of driving performance improvements that reach beyond the scope of individual learning activities. As a learning organization knowledge and skills build throughout the organization even outside of formal learning activities.

The Role of eLearning in the Workplace

The importance of workplace learning in the modern, dynamic competitive environment is a set condition regardless of the delivery method for that learning. Elearning, however, delivers several advantages and is uniquely aligned with the identified preferences and motivations for worker engagement in the learning process. To satisfy those motivations elearning needs to be deliberately designed and assessed, and also integrated into the overall strategic approach of the firm.

As discussed earlier, learners in the workplace want to improve their skills and engage in learning activities that directly benefit their day-to-day work. Elearning is uniquely positioned to do this by linking the learning activities directly to the work and, through this close connection with the learner's responsibilities, motivating better engagement and retention than other delivery mechanisms (David, Selleh, & Iahad, 2012). Elearning also has the advantage of providing users with greater control of the learning experience in many different aspects. Providing greater control to the users increases both their satisfaction and motivation in the learning experience (Cheng, Wang, Yang, & Kinshuk, 2011).

This potential for increased learner motivation and satisfaction means that elearning is more than just an alternative method of delivery. In many situations elearning may be the preferred delivery mechanism for workplace learning. This preference is of course dependent on the individual learners and the content of the instruction, but used properly the method has definite advantages. To capitalize on these advantages, however, the design of the elearning experience must be properly executed (see *Figure 4*).

Workplace elearning design begins at the foundation of the firm. As explored earlier it is critical for an organization, beginning with management, to support the learning activities and learning environment for employees. In the context of elearning specifically, Cheng, Wang, Moorman, Olaniran, and Chen (2012) explain that before investing in an elearning program management must eliminate organizational

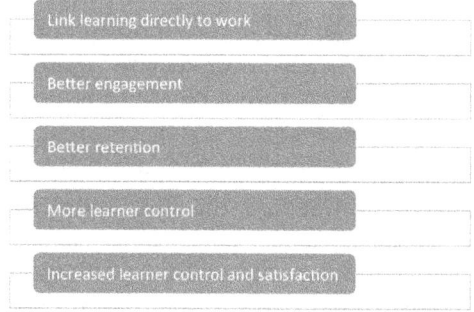

Figure 4. Advantages in developing quality online courses.

barriers and create a positive learning environment that also provides an appropriate reward system. This early engagement of management involves more than just establishing the organizational structure; it also helps to align the content of the learning experience with the needs of the firm.

Both workers and managers have an interest in a learning experience contributing to the workers' ability to perform better. Linking this to the design of elearning can create an environment of performance-based learning, where the goal is establish learning objectives and engage the learner in a process that achieves those set objectives (Wang, Vogel, & Ran, 2011). The actual delivery of the learning experience should be closely linked to the learning needs of workers. For elearning design in the workplace this means utilizing andragogy and self-directed learning (Cheng, Wang, Yang, & Kinshuk, 2011).

The design aspects of workplace elearning are clearly a critical step in building a successful learning experience for the employees. For the firm there also needs to be a clear advantage to providing the learning opportunity to employees. When using elearning as a platform this means making a clear connection between elearning themes and workplace learning requirements. This is necessary because the real purpose of a workplace elearning initiative is for the firm to generate positive results in employee behavior and overall performance (Cheng, Wang, Yang, & Kinshuk, 2011).

Connecting elearning to the needs of the workplace goes beyond just the goals and objectives and includes the application of appropriate theories for the environment. "Theories specific to workplace learning can be categorized into four groups: adult learning, organization learning, Community of Practice (CoP), and knowledge management" (Wang, 2011). With so many different elements combining to create a successful workplace elearning experience an organization must be deliberate in their approach to the process. This involves including elearning as a component of the overall strategic plan for the firm.

For a workplace elearning effort to deliver the expected positive results it must begin with a sound plan. This plan is based on a business and people-centered strategy (Wang, Vogel, & Ran, 2011). The planning process, as part of a firm's overall strategic plan, is critical in today's business environment. The increasingly dynamic competitive environment has forced firms to focus on how they can establish sustainable competitive advantage and one of those approaches, the improvement of their workers, is increasingly achieved through the use of elearning (Cheng, Wang, Yang, & Kinshuk, 2011). This strategic focus on worker development was reflected in the study by Cheng, Wang, Morch, Chen, Kinshuk, and Specter (2014) where they identified two of the four dimensions of workplace elearning as elearning for continuing education and professional development and the integration of knowledge management with elearning.

As knowledge workers increasingly become the engine of productivity and competitive advantage in the knowledge economy the development of those workers is of increasing importance to a firm's overall strategy. This drives the importance of workplace elearning, as, "Studies have also demonstrated a relation between the prevalence of ICTs (information communication technologies) at work and the rate of workplace learning" (David, Selleh, & Iahad, 2012). With worker development a premium concern for competitive companies, and worker development aided by the use of elearning approaches, elearning by extension is a component of creating and maintaining competitive advantage for the modern firm.

Because elearning is an important element of a firm's overall strategic plan the final element in its planning and implementation is the use of assessment. In workplace learning assessment this often takes the form of Key Performance Indicators (KPIs). Rather than assessing the learning process directly, KPIs assess the critical areas of individual and organizational performance that contribute to overall firm success (Wang, Vogel, & Ran, 2011). This approach, rather than simply measuring employees' academic mastery of course content, examines the degree of positive impact that occurs following the training. Ultimately this information can be utilized to share knowledge and build a learning community in the firm (Wang, Vogel, & Ran, 2011).

This systematic approach to workplace elearning, from the first steps of matching the learning environment to learner motivations and establishing a learning culture to assessing the impact of the elearning efforts on organizational performance makes the application of elearning in the workplace unique. At its core, however, the process of planning, executing, and assessing the learning is very similar to how elearning is planned and deployed in any environment. The difference in the workplace is the clear strategic focus on bottom line performance. As such, workplace elearning must be developed from the beginning as a performance-oriented process that will deliver measurable performance outcomes.

Conclusion

Workplace learning is a key to success for the modern firm. It goes beyond the concept of simple training events and is focused on developing the capacity of employees throughout the company to perform better, to improve their own knowledge, skills, and careers, and through those individual improvements to drive positive change and success for the firm as a whole. The process is no longer an isolated practice or something that is limited to only the HR group, but a strategic imperative for every part of a company. Increasingly the mechanism for this effort is workplace elearning. The online environment delivers opportunities to employees that are beyond those of traditional classroom-based training events and also brings additional benefits to the organization. Regardless of delivery format, motivated employees, positive learning cultures, and a dedication to sound practice are what will drive success for the modern firm.

References

Aragon, M., Jimenez, D., & Valle, R. (2014). Training and performance: The mediating role of organizational learning. *Business Research Quarterly*, 17, p 161-173.

Batalla-Busquets, J. & Pacheco-Bernal, C. (2013). On-the-job elearning: Workers' attitudes and perceptions. *International Review of Research in Open and Distributed Learning*, 14(1), Retrieved from: http://www.irrodl.org/index.php/irrodl/article/view/1304/2417.

Billet, S. & Choi, S. (2013). Learning through work: Emerging perspectives and new challenges. *Journal of Workplace learning*, 25(4), p 264-276.

Cheng, B, Wang, M., Moormann, J., Olaniran, B., & Chen, N. (2012). The effects of organizational learning environment factors on elearning acceptance. *Computers & Education*, 58, p 885-899.

Cheng, B., Wang, M., Morch, A., Chen, N., Kinshuk, P., & Spector, J. (2014). Research on elearning in the workplace 2000-2012: A bibliometric analysis of the literature. *Educational Research Review*, 11, 56-72.

Cheng, B., Wang, M., Yang, S., & Kinshuk, P. (2011). Acceptance of competency-based workplace elearning systems: effects of individual and peer learning support. *Computers & Education*, 57(1), 1317-1333.

David, O., Salleh, M., & Iahad, N. (2012). The impact of elearning in workplace: Focus on organizations and healthcare environments. *International Arab Journal of e-Technology*, 2(4), 203-209.

Govaerts, N., Kyndt, E., Dochy, F., & Baert, H. (2010). Influence of learning and working climate on the retention of talented employees. *Journal of Workplace learning*, 23(1), p 35-55.

Harmon, P. (2015). The scope and evolution of business process management. In J. vom Brocke & M. Rosemann (Eds.); *Handbook on Business Process Management 1, International Handbooks on Information Systems*, Springer-Verlag, Berlin Heidelberg. Kyndt, E. & Baert, H. (2013). Antecedents of employees' involvement in work-related learning: A systematic review. *Review of Educational Research*, 83(2), p 273-313.

Kyndt, E., Govaerts, N., Keunen, L., & Dochy, F. (2012). Examining the learning intentions of low-qualified employees: a mixed method study. *Journal of Workplace learning*, 25(3), p 178-197.

Kyndt, E., Raes, E., Dochy, F., & Janssens, E. (2012). Approaches to learning at work: Investigating work motivation, perceived workload, and choice independence. *Journal of Career Development*, 40(4), p 271-291.

McQuaid, R., Raeside, R., Canduela, J., Egdell, V., & Lindsay, C. (2012). Engaging low skilled employees in workplace learning. *UK Commission for Employment and Skills*.

Minbaeva, D., Pedersen, T., Bjorkman, I., Fey, C., & Park, H. (2014). MNC knowledge transfer, subsidiary absorbtive capacity, and HRM. *Journal of International Business Studies*, 45, p 38-51.

Pantouvakis, A. & Bouranta, N. (2013). The link between organizational learning culture and customer satisfaction: Confirming relationship and exploring moderating effect. *The Learning organization*, 20(1), p 48-64.

Simmons, S. (2011). The origins and descriptions of ADDIE. Retrieved from: http://www.shelbyesimmons.me/uploads/1/0/4/1/10414302/simmonsseaddiepaper.pdf.

Sung, S. & Choi, J. (2014). Do organizations spend wisely on employees? Effects of training and development investments on learning and innovation in organizations. *Journal of Organizational Behavior*, 35, p 393-412.

Wang, M. (2011). Integrating organizational, social, and individual perspectives in Web 2.0-based workplace elearning. *Information Systems Frontiers*, 13(2), p 191-205.

Wang, M., Vogel, D., & Ran, W. (2011). Creating a performance-oriented elearning environment: A design science approach. *Information and Management*, 48(7), 260-269.

Definitions

ADDIE model: An instructional design process model consisting of Analysis, Design, Develop, Implement, and Evaluation

competitive environment: The market in which an organization offers its products or services to customers also pursued by other organizations

elearning: The process of obtaining new information through a digital medium key performance indicators (KPIs): Measurable elements of an organization's operations that link to successful outcomes

learning organization: An organization that has sufficient processes and resources to continuously generate and retain new knowledge

stakeholders: Individuals or organizations impacted by an organization's actions and performance

workplace learning: The acquisition of new information or sk.

3 Questions for an Online Leader
Dr. Phil Ice
Vice President of Research and Development, American Public University System

My Thoughts on Re-envisioning Online Teaching and Learning

Dr. Phil Ice is the vice president of research and development for American Public University System. For over a decade, Ice's research has focused on the impact of new and emerging technologies on cognition in online learning environments. Work in this area has brought him international recognition in the form of four Sloan-C Effective Practice of the Year Awards (2007, 2009, 2010 and 2013) as well as the esteemed Gomory Award for Data Driven Quality Improvement in 2009. He has been recognized by industry through membership in Adobe's Education Leaders Group and Adobe's Higher Education Advisory Board, as well as a recipient of the Adobe Higher Education Leaders Impact Award in 2010. Ice's vision for the future of technology in higher education has also been demonstrated by his inclusion on the advisory council for the 2011 NMC / ELI Horizon Report and his role as Principal Investigator on a $1.05 million WICHE/WCET grant to explore online retention patterns across six institutions. His work has covered the use of technology mediated feedback, which has been adopted by over 50 institutions of higher education in five countries, multi-level institutional assessment techniques, learning analytics and application of semantic analysis for mapping institutional learning assets. Ice has also worked with seven other researchers in the United States and Canada in numerous other research initiatives related to the Community of Inquiry Framework. This research has resulted in the development of a validated instrument that captures the intersection of Teaching, Social and Cognitive presence in online learning environments.

I had the opportunity to sit down with this issue's "3 Questions for an Online Leader" to speak with him about his accomplishments as well as to find out more about his visions for online learning and current projects he is involved with.

Question 1. Dr. Ice, so I am very familiar with your research on using the Community of Inquiry framework for online teaching and learning, but what have you been involved in lately?

Ice: *One of the big projects I became engaged with after the initial flurry of activity around the CoI was Learning Analytics. I got involved with that early on, I would say. At APUS we started looking at how we could use big data to predict retention in the same way that sports uses analytics to handicap an event or marketing agencies use analytics to predict customer trends. From there I approached the Bill and Melinda Gates Foundation about getting a group of universities together and see if we could aggregate multi-institutional data sets and look for trends. That resulted in funding for the Predictive Analytics Reporting (PAR) Framework and later as one of the inspirational factors that led to the founding of f Civitas.*

doi: 10.18278/il.4.2.6

Since then I've moved on to work with rich learning environments that can be delivered on mobile as well as the desktop. As you know, this journal was the inspiration for what is now being done with course apps at APUS and an increasing number of other institutions. That's what is consuming all of my time now and I must say its quite exciting.

Question 2. This is obviously a new evolution for online teaching and learning. What changes or shifts do you foresee as a result of this evolution?

Ice: *First, I would have to say that it's probably as much of a revolution as an evolution; and one that is much overdue at that. When you look at what we provide our students, in terms of a learning experience, very little has changed since the inception of online learning. It's still a very flat, text-centric experience that is not at all stimulating for the student. In stark contrast, they engage with rich, online experiences everyday in their personal lives and then are condemned to engage with outdated experiences when they enter the classroom. Some older students are still willing to accept this because they are of an age where they knew a world that wasn't fully digital, however, younger learners, especially Gen Z aren't going to accept what we have to offer. They are going to laugh at us. So if higher education wants to remain relevant, we have to adapt. I think that's what we are doing with course apps, or at least trying to do. We are providing rich, interactive experiences that engage learners with a look and feel that is aligned with contemporary experiences.*

In some ways this is a heavy lift for institutions. They are being forced to rethink everything about how they engage students and what the implications are for both faculty and infrastructure. I believe though that this is the beginning of serious differentiation among institutions. Of course the top 300 will always survive, but for everyone else I believe that those who adopt this type of approach will separate themselves from everyone else and it will be this group that doesn't just survive, but thrive. Further, its not just a matter of differentiation and survival, it's just the right thing to do. We have the ability to create incredible learning experiences and if we don't do it then I think we need to consider why we are in higher education to start with.

With respect to models and underlying theory, well I think we are making that up as we go and there's nothing wrong with that. When online learning first emerged the CoI was made up to explain what was happening. Some of it was based on grounded theory in traditional learning environments and some of it was based upon what we discovered about how the environment impacted cognition, interaction, etc. The same is true now. I believe we have foundational elements, including the CoI that will still apply, albeit in pieces and then there are things we are seeing that will have to be researched and explained. The models are definitely changing and that's really exciting to me.

Question 3. Undoubtedly, you've had several innovative ideas in the world of online education throughout your professional career. What fuels, or inspires you to come up with such innovation?

Ice: *Simply put, I'm a dreamer. I guess I'm lucky enough to be one of those people who managed to muddle their way through our K-12 and higher education institutions without being completely stripped of creativity. To me, the art of the possible is the most exciting thing there is. Being able to continually think about what can be instead of what is gives me hope. That's part of my everyday life, but it has special meaning in my professional life because I see how many more people can be positively impacted if we can deliver on the adjacent possible. When I get tired of trying to do that, or when it becomes obvious that the field is no longer interested in the possible, then I know it's time for me to find something else to do. So far I've been lucky enough that that hasn't happened. The downside is that you frequently rub a lot of people the wrong way when you continuously dream, but so far I've been able to find a handful of others who are willing to embrace an idea that everyone else considers crazy and help me run with it.*

The Tangible and Intangible Benefits of Offering Massive Open Online Courses: Faculty Perspectives

Credence Baker,[A] Fred Nafukho,[B] Karen McCaleb,[C] Melissa Becker,[D] and Michelle Johnson[E]

The primary purpose of this study was to establish perceptions of faculty members regarding the benefits of Massive Open Online Courses (MOOCs) in higher education. In addition, the study sought to determine what the challenges of offering MOOCs were and what accounted for the low completion rates of MOOCs. Data were collected using an online survey from 1,057 faculty members in a major university system based in the southern United States. Of the 1,057 target faculty population who completed the online survey, 939 responses were viable, and only 396 of the faculty respondents provided answers to the open-ended question regarding the benefits of MOOCs. Overall, the researchers analyzed 396 faculty responses using the Atlas Ti qualitative program. Open-ended coding was conducted to determine what key concepts faculty provided in their responses to describe the benefits of MOOCs. Axial codes were developed to group primary codes into broader concepts which enabled the researchers to create themes based on the axial codes. The responses provide rich and robust descriptions about the benefits and drawbacks of MOOCs. The paper presents the results of the open-ended question.

Keywords: *MOOCs, massive open online courses, higher education, online education, distance learning*

[A] **Dr. Credence Baker** is an assistant professor and assistant graduate dean at Tarleton State University.

[B] **Fredrick Muyia Nafukho** serves as Professor and Department Head in the Department of Educational Administration and Human Resource Development, College of Education and Human Development at Texas A&M University. Dr. Nafukho earned his Ph.D. in Human Resource & Leadership Development from Louisiana State University, M.Ed in Economics of Education and B.Ed in Business Studies and Economics from Kenyatta University, Kenya. He attended Harvard's Management Development Program (MDP) offered by Harvard Institutes for Higher Education. He joined the Department of Educational Administration and Human Resource Development at Texas A&M University as an Associate Professor in August 2007. Dr. Nafukho has received numerous awards in recognition of his scholarship including: the Fulbright Scholarship in 1996, Distinguished International Scholar Award, Louisiana State University in 1997, Arkansas Business Teacher Educator of the Year Award in 2004, Cutting Edge Award for the Outstanding Papers, Academy of Human Resource Development (with his student Dr. Carroll C. Graham) in 2005 and Outstanding New Faculty Award, CEHD at Texas A&M University in 2008. Dr. Nafukho's research foci is on adult learning, emotional intelligence and leadership development, organizational learning, performance improvement, evaluation in organizations, and investment in human capital development.

doi: 10.18278/il.4.2.8

Introduction

The need to transform the way university leaders think and run their institutions, especially in this technology-driven learning environment, has become more pronounced in the 21st century than ever before (Clark, 1998; Nafukho & Wawire, 2004; Ziderman & Albrecht, 1995). On the significant role of technology in higher education, Miller (2014, p. 1) noted, "Most students graduating from college in the present era will experience at least some part of their education via technology, whether as an enhancement to the traditional, face-to-face approach, fully online or some mix of the two." The academic institution has changed and evolved based on its consumer needs as well as the available societal resources. One such resource which has altered common educational practice has been the rapid surge of technology. A new challenge for academia is determining the technology tools best suited to provide strong pedagogical practices to a technology-savvy population. As new technologies emerge, and student needs shift, universities search for ways to support student learning and growth. In addition, university leaders and professors are challenged to develop entrepreneurial ways of delivering educational products and services to their students (Nafukho & Muyia, 2014).

Today, technology is commonplace. First-year college freshmen have lived with cell phone technology, Internet, and social media. Students can watch movies, listen to music, conduct banking business, and communicate with an unlimited number of people through personal cell phones. As a result of the technological impact on society, our higher education delivery system has also morphed. An increasing number of universities and campuses are offering distance education courses as a result of this shift. According to the National Governor's Association, "the number of students taking an online course has nearly quadrupled over the past decade, with nearly one-third of all postsecondary students in the nation – including many working adults – currently taking at least one course online" (NGA, 2013, p.1). This information is corroborated by the Sloan Foundation's 2010 Survey of Online Learning assertion that more than 30% of all students take at least one online course during their college career (Hachey, Wladis, & Conway, 2012). Although the term "distance education" has historically meant "correspondence course", today that definition is more inclusive.

Distance Education (DE) has been implemented in the United States for several decades. The evolution of DE has typically been classified by the technology as well as the pedagogical approach utilized. Anderson and Dron (2012) summarized the three generations of the technology used as: 1) postal correspondence; 2) mass media of television, radio and film production; and 3) interactive technologies. Although the generations are each unique, they overlap and intertwine.

No matter the learning modality or grade level, a common challenge for teachers is student engagement (Jensen, 2005). Educators today must create instructional

---

[C] **Dr. Karen McCaleb** is an associate professor and associate dean of the College of Education at Texas A&M Corpus Christi.

[D] **Dr. Melissa Becker** is an associate professor of education at Tarleton State University.

[E] **Michelle Johnson** is a doctoral student in the College of Education at Texas A&M University.

opportunities by utilizing technology to empower learners to solve problems, access information, and create relationships outside the classroom using the digital tools (November, 2010). In the online environment, this challenge is exacerbated by several factors, including the lack of face-to-face contact, a hindered ability to share emotions like enthusiasm, encouragement or concern, learner/instructor isolation, and the unrealistic expectations of students that online coursework is easier and requires less time (Cull, Reed, & Kirk, 2010). These challenges are likely further compounded in a Massive Open Online Course (MOOC), where the sheer number of students lessen the ability of the instructor to engage individual students, and can manifest into high withdraw/dropout rates in MOOCs, as reported by Koutropoulos and Hougue (2012). Jordan (2013) found that the average MOOC course is found to enroll around 43,000 students, 6.5% of whom complete the course. Despite these challenges, the online learning environment has unique components for fostering student engagement and learning, including flexibility, interactivity, and creativity for online instructors to generate a variety of learning experiences that are both structural and pedagogical in nature.

The flexibility of learning anytime/anywhere can empower students to take charge of their own learning, and focus on important intellectual tasks at optimal times. Flexibility of learning has been cited as a major factor in the sustained growth of online courses over ten years from less than 2 million in the early 2000s to 6.7 million in the fall of 2011 as reported in *Changing Course: Ten Years of Tracking Online Education in the United States* (Allen & Seaman, 2013). Additionally, online courses afford a unique platform for interactivity, collaboration, and community building using tools like discussion boards, blogs, wikis, collaborative documents/presentations, and social media groups. When carefully scaffolded by the instructor, these activities can allow for rich communication and collaboration, as well as creativity to build upon ideas and projects using the vast resources of the Internet. Moreover, the Internet allows students to connect with experts in the field, and bring in perspectives from outside of the online classroom.

Finally, online instructors can call upon imagery, audio, video, music, and interactive elements to enhance the design of an online course, and express creativity in the design of instruction for online students. In terms of pedagogical strategies for engaging online students, the online learning environment allows instructors to establish course goals and relevance and clearly communicate expectations before the course begins, and at each assessment benchmark during the semester. Because of the 'backwards design' of an online course, and the necessity to view it through the learner's lens, an online instructor can set online students up for success through organization and good design. Communication can be enhanced in an online course through behaviors congruent with immediacy and presence, both of which have been shown to enhance student engagement (Richardson & Swan, 2003; Witt, Wheeless, & Allen, 2004). Online instructors can use asynchronous tools like email and discussion boards, and synchronous tools like chat, Skype or Google Hangouts to connect with and support students. Finally, online learning environments allow for multiple forms of formative and summative assessment. Online instructors can provide timely feedback in written/text form, as well in audio/video format.

Purpose of the Study

Although delivering learning content online is associated with numerous advantages, Massive Open Online Courses with thousands of students enrolled have faced scepticism; especially from faculty members based in major research universities. When it comes to learning, both high-tech (online learning) and high-touch (face-to-face learning) issues become important, especially to faculty members involved in the design and delivery of face-to-face, blended and online learning. In terms of engaging students in the learning process, it has been established that utilizing a mix of face-to-face and online instruction promotes optimal learning (Bonk, 2002). While MOOCs are now becoming a reality in higher education, limited studies have been conducted, especially among faculty members regarding their perceptions on the learning effectiveness of MOOCs. The primary purpose of this study was to establish perceptions of faculty regarding the benefits of MOOCs in a major southern university system in the United States.

Conceptual Framework

Anderson and Dron (2012) have offered a broader view of distance education by classifying the three generations by the type of pedagogical approach employed. The three theoretical frameworks are termed: cognitive/behaviorist, social constructivist, and connectivist. The following synopsis of the three pedagogical frameworks provide a broad overview of this distance education technology development.

The first phase, or generation of technology adoption in course delivery was that of postal correspondence. This concept was popular during much of the 20th century and used the postal service as its technological means of exchanging communication and between instructor and student. In this course delivery system, one instructor could instruct and communicate with one student or several students in different locations. This instructional method utilized a cognitive/behaviorist approach in which the focus is on the individual learner. No longer was it imperative for students to travel to a campus to receive instruction. Through this type of distance education, students in more rural areas or who faced other barriers in accessing a college campus were able to pursue higher education. Obvious limitations to this method of instructional delivery include the time students and faculty had to wait between correspondences, and the lack of interactivity between students.

As technology advanced, so did the ways in which it was utilized by institutions of higher education. The second generation of technology development utilized a social constructivist pedagogical approach. In this delivery system, student-to-student and student-to-instructor communication opportunities were expanded and emphasized. Through technology, such as email and the World Wide Web, the course environment became more interactive and dynamic. Unlike the first generation of technology use in higher education which primarily provided instructional information in an isolated situation, this generation attempts to provide students an online class environment in which they can build a virtual classroom community.

The third generation, utilizing a connectivist approach, is even more entrenched in social networks. This informal learning approach, relies on the interactions between students as they use technology tools such tweets, blogs, and social media. Unlike the first generation, this educational experience relies on students working together to help each other as individuals, and as teams, to learn and use a personal learning network (PLN). The constructivist approach has been utilized in the design and delivery of xMOOCs and cMOOCs. The xMOOCs refer to instructor-guided lessons which include discussion forums, videos, and encourage discussion among learners. cMOOCs, on the other hand, are based on connectivism where learners engage in self-paced learning as they navigate the course, build a web of connections among fellow learners and create meaning by setting their own learning goals and choosing how to engage in the learning process. Through active engagement and active learning communities, the learners in cMOOCs learn and create knowledge together (Scholz, 2013).

Literature Review

As evident from the technology evolution in higher education, course delivery systems must adapt to society's needs and student preferences. Institutions of higher education have evolved from postal correspondence to providing an online learning experience that parallels the design of an on-campus class. However, as a result of the increasing possibilities of technology infusion in education, academia is now challenging the concept of the traditional online class design by offering courses in a very nontraditional manner. The development of Massive Open Online Courses is rooted within the ideals of openness in education, knowledge should be shared freely, and the desire to learn should be met without demographic, economic, and geographical constraints (Yuan & Powell, 2013). This idealized view of MOOCs posits that benefits of online learning can be offered on a massive scale. Leckart (2012) heralded [the advent of MOOCs] as a significant event in shaping the future of higher education, envisioning a future where MOOCs offer full degrees as 'bricks and mortar' institutions decline. According to the Oxford Dictionary (2013), the term MOOC is defined as "a course of study made available over the Internet without charge to a very large number of people." The courses are typically free, but historically institutions have not allowed participants to receive actual course credit. However, as MOOCs have become more mainstream, universities are beginning to explore ways to reverse this trend. For example, Arizona State University (ASU), the largest public university in the United States, recently launched it's Global Freshman Academy in partnership with MOOC provider edX, allowing anyone to take an entire first year of college online via MOOCs for free ASU transcript credit. MIT recently announced its intent to allow students to obtain one of its master's degrees by doing half of the coursework via MOOCs. A 2015 U.S. and World News Report lists similar MOOC-for-credit initiatives at institutions like Georgia Institute of Technology and The University of Illinois – Urbana-Champaign.

The first cMOOC was offered in 2008, by the University of Manitoba in Canada. The course, *Connectivism and Connective Knowledge*, registered twenty-five paying students seeking course credit as well as 2,300 other students, from the public, who enrolled at no cost. Daniel (2012), a well-known scholar of MOOCs, observed that Stanford University offered a free MOOCs course on Artificial Intelligence, which enrolled 160,000 students. The success of this MOOC course motivated Sebastian Thrun, the professor at Stanford University who developed the course to establish a MOOC private start-up company called Udacity which has played an important role of promoting the development of MOOCs in other universities (Meyer, 2012). Yuan and Powell (2013) stated that present-day MOOCs are generating considerable media attention and significant interest from higher education institutions as well as venture capitalists who see a lucrative business opportunity. MOOCs can be seen as an extension of existing online learning approaches, in terms of open access to courses and scalability, but also offer an opportunity to think afresh about new business learning models that include elements of open education. Since the first MOOC course was offered in 2008, over ten MOOC companies have been established in partnership with world-renowned universities including: Class 2 Go, Cousera, Cousesites, edX, Google Course Builder, Instructure Canvas, Khan Academy, NOVOEd, OpenMOOC, Udacity and Udemy, with many others in development.

Other lenses through which to view MOOCs include the political sector, where government leaders see the potential to address the problem of higher education budget constraints and lower the cost of degree courses by enabling inexpensive, low-risk experiments in different forms of higher education provision (Carey, 2013). The private business sector envisions MOOCs as a way to enter the higher education market by providing a MOOC platform and developing partnerships with existing institutions and to explore new delivery models in higher education (Yuan & Powell, 2013). Advocates see MOOCs as a disruptive innovation that will transform higher education. To these varied lenses, MOOCs provide a powerful tool to make fundamental changes in the organization and delivery of higher education over the next decade (Shirky, 2012). Most of the writings on MOOCs have been presented in mainstream newspapers and refereed academic journals. There exists a gap in the literature on faculty perspectives of MOOCs, hence the need to involve faculty with regard to the design and successful delivery of MOOCs.

Research Questions

To achieve the purpose of the study, the following research questions guided the study:

1. What are faculty perceptions regarding the benefits of Massive Open Online Courses in higher education?
2. What are the challenges of offering MOOCs in your institution?
3. What accounts for the low completion rates of MOOCs?

In order to achieve the purpose of this study and answer the research questions, a cross-sectional survey was utilized to collect and analyze data from the study respondents. This being an exploratory descriptive study, a cross-sectional survey design was employed to enable the researchers to capture faculty perceptions regarding the benefits of MOOCs. Thus, a self-perception survey was selected as the instrument to collect data since self-reporting has been found to be the most direct and common way to establish study participant perceptions (Anderson & Kanuka, 1997). Dillman (2000) also observed that self-reports serve the interest of study participants who, in this case, were faculty who were typically teaching using face-to-face, online or blended methods. In their teaching role, faculty members serve as experts who direct the learning process, and are critical in encouraging students to learn for a lifetime through continuing professional education. Hence the need to determine their perception of MOOCs which are mainly taken by learners who already have first degrees and are interested in continuing professional education (Cull, Reed, & Kirk, 2010).

Target Population and Sample

The target population for the study was comprised of 7,000 faculty members employed by a major university system based in the southern portion of the United States. Of the 7,000 targeted population of faculty, 1,057 (15.1%) of system faculty completed the online survey, and of those who completed the survey 939 (88.8%) of the responses were complete and usable. The researchers of this study, however report the results pertaining to the open-ended responses which sought answers to the three research questions. Only 396 of the faculty respondents provided answers to the open-ended questions regarding their perceptions of the benefits of MOOCs, challenges facing MOOCs and why there were low completion rates in MOOCs. Overall, the researchers analyzed 396 faculty responses using the Atlas Ti qualitative program. The sample included 46% females and 54% males. Eighty-two percent of the respondents identified themselves as Caucasian, 8% Hispanic, 2% African American, 1% Asian, 1% American Indian, and 6% who identified as "other". Sixty-seven percent of the sample indicated they were tenured or tenure track faculty, while 33% said they were non-tenure track.

Open-ended coding was conducted to determine what key concepts faculty provided in their responses to describe the benefits and drawbacks of MOOCs, challenges of MOOCs and reasons for the low completion rates in MOOCs courses. Axial codes were developed to group primary codes into broader concepts which enabled the researchers to create themes based on the axial codes.

Instrumentation

The electronic survey was comprised of several validated instrument items which have been used to measure perceptions regarding MOOCs. The researchers of this study obtained permission from the Babson Survey Research Group, a renowned research team in the area of online learning, to use some of the questionnaire items from what was originally known as the Sloan Online Survey, through a partnership with the Sloan Consortium and Pearson. The other items of the instrument were adapted from Anderson and Kanuka's (1997) work and were modified to meet the needs of this study. In addition, items were obtained from Ke's (2011) study. Only the results for the open-ended section of the instrument are reported in this study.

Data Collection Procedures

Prior to data collection and to protect human subjects in the study, the approval to conduct this study was obtained from the Institutional Review Boards (IRBs) of the three institutions where the researchers are employed. Once the IRB permissions were granted, the researchers worked with a main contact person in the university system of over ten institutions to coordinate the data collection process. Data delimiters were identified by the researchers to ensure confidentiality of data. From a list provided by the university contact, survey invitations were distributed via e-mail. In the invitation, a unique link was provided and directed the participants to the study. The electronic survey was created in such a way that participants could only complete the survey one time.

Data Analysis

To analyze the qualitative data collected through open-ended questions from the 396 faculty members who provided rich and detailed explanations on the benefits of MOOCs, the researchers transcribed the survey responses into a readable format with the Atlas Ti qualitative program. The researchers conducted open coding to determine what key concepts faculty members discussed to describe their MOOCs experience or inexperience. Next, axial codes were developed to group primary codes into broader concepts. Themes emerged based on these axial codes. The researchers discussed findings and verified the coding and themes to develop a working knowledge of the study participants' experience or inexperience with MOOCs.

Results

Survey participants were asked the open ended question, "What are the benefits of offering MOOCs?" The qualitative data from this section of the survey was unitized and then coded, thus revealing five major categories along with some subcategories on who benefits from institutions offering MOOCs. In addition to discussing the benefits, participants also discussed some of the drawbacks of offering MOOCs although they were not asked to provide information on drawbacks. This was an unexpected finding as participants were specifically asked about the benefits. This section of the paper discusses the student benefits, institution or program benefits, and the reported drawbacks of offering MOOCs.

Student Benefits

According to Newman (2013), individuals may be motivated to enroll in adult education courses to gain control of their lives, learn to reason freely, nurture their consciousness, participate in a civil society, or learn how to better assert themselves in their world. While the motive to enroll in a MOOC is unique to the individual, the benefits offered by MOOCs are extended to all students.

Access to education. Among these benefits are a large number of individuals having access to education, one participant stated that by offering MOOCs institutions provide "accessibility to [educational courses] to a diverse and wide-ranging student body". While another participant noted, MOOCs provide "accessibility to students who could benefit from foundational courses without incurring an additional financial burden." One respondent also reported that traditional education is available to "only the "elite" or upper middle class or students willing to "mortgage their future with financial aid" can afford higher education with the traditional four years of face-to-face campus attendance".

Flexibility in education. MOOCs offer students convenience and flexibility in attending college courses. One participant noted students are able to enroll in courses which are "better fitting in their schedules because they render time of day for coursework irrelevant". Meaning, students are able to attend classes and complete course work without feeling the constraints of working, family obligations, or having to travel long distances.

Self-paced learning with no grade pressure. Participants stated students benefit greatly from the self-paced learning environment offered by MOOCs. This environment, as noted by one participant, offers "bite-sized, self-paced instruction with experts". While another participant stated, MOOCs are "self-paced, capitalize on developing and sharing knowledge, skills, and abilities to many [students] by leveraging the expertise of the few".

Students are able to learn from the experts at their own pace without feeling the pressure to make good grades. One participant noted MOOCs as "giving a safe environment for testing technical skills without a grade being on the line". Thus, students are able to learn without the added stress of making a good grade which may affect their ability to learn. The benefits MOOCs offer students are enhanced by the many benefits institutions and programs gain from offering MOOCs.

Institution and Program Benefits

Institutions and programs benefits greatly from the marketing aspect related to offering MOOCs. One participant stated "if well-designed and conducted, a MOOC can raise the visibility of the institution and of the instructor". Thus, having well-designed and conducted courses generates publicity and increases the visibility of the institution or program on the national level. Participants also noted if institutions are highly visible, they then have the ability to broaden their recruiting to reach a wide diversity of students.

Reaching a wide audience. MOOCs provide institutions and programs the opportunity to reach students who may be dispersed across the country by offering flexibility in location. One participant stated institutions are "reaching geographically remote and economically disadvantaged curious learners". Students are not required to be geographically housed in the same location as the institution or program they attend. Meaning, institutions and programs are able to electronically reach new, larger student populations without being limited by physical space and by removing the barrier that distance can create. The ability to reach a wider audience challenges institutions or programs to improve course quality and provide professional development.

Improving course quality. Participants noted that the quality of courses can be improved through the use of MOOCs. By offering a course online, instructors are challenged to be creative in designing and delivering instruction. As one participant noted, "when creatively and thoughtfully produced, the MOOC provides greater attention to the visual presentation needed to capture interest and enhance learning" for the students. The ability of instructors to create interactive, engaging online MOOCs also "promulgates best practices" as noted by one participant.

Professional development for professors and teachers. As instructors seek to provide the highest quality of content for their courses to students, MOOCs also provide opportunities for faculty professional development. Participants noted MOOCs are a means to offer professional development to faculty teaching at smaller institutions who may experience limitations on travel or availability of funding. One participant stated "professional continuing education MOOCs provide opportunities to people in smaller communities who may not have access to F2F CE opportunities". Thus, faculty members gain access to professional development opportunities that are flexible in location and scheduling.

Multiple Benefits from Offering MOOCs

MOOCs help students and instructors overcome the barriers of distance and high costs as well as the time constraints associated with the traditional college and professional development courses. By providing a flexible learning and teaching alternative, institutions and programs are better able to market themselves, serve geographically remote and financially disadvantaged populations, and promote best teaching practices without having to increase the physical size of their campuses.

Overall, the participants stated MOOCs offer a wide variety of benefits. However, even without prompting on the survey, some participants noted drawbacks of MOOCs.

The Drawbacks of offering MOOCs

One of the major of concerns for any institution offering courses, face-to-face or online, are completion rates. Participants in this study noted that for MOOCs, specifically, the completion rate is roughly 5% due to many students enrolling in a course and then dropping out. This low completion rate may seemingly reflect that MOOCs, as noted by participants, offer a very low level of educational benefits or may be seen as a supplement to teaching and not the primary means of delivering course content.

Faculty who participated in this study suggested that MOOCs "online offering effectiveness is limited to teaching definitions and for reinforcement practice" as there are some courses that simply and logically cannot be taught online. Reflecting this sentiment, one participant stated, "A simple example is swimming. Few people will learn how to swim by taking an online course" and suggested that this example can be extrapolated to many other fields of study.

According to participants, these drawbacks and limitations also impact how students perceive MOOCs. Because of the lack of pressure to achieve high grades (a cited benefit by some participants), students may view MOOCs as optional entertainment rather than an academically rigorous course. However, another participant suggested that the limitations of MOOCs may relate to the student's motivation. This participant noted "if the user [student] is not motivated (i.e., use of the MOOC format is coerced), then the benefits of MOOCs are zilch". The lack of motivation by students may provide insight into the mixed results universities may receive on student success. As one faculty participant explained, "universities across the country are having mixed results. They will not necessarily be "better" or "worse", but like any course, it will depend on the structure of the course and learning styles of the participants".

Yet, the lack of motivation on the instructor's behalf to create an engaging MOOC course design may be explained by an instructor's previous experience with and preference for another online course program. One participant explained preference for another online program in the following response:

> I teach many online courses and have since 2001 and I have been closely following the professional development issue. MOOCs are useful if offered entirely freely online, but as a replacement for actual courses (online, with regular caps of 25-30, or face-to-face) they are worse than useless as current studies are showing. However, I strongly support [online program].

Instructors who have spent several years teaching may have experience with other online course programs and find those may yield more success for students than MOOCs.

Whether the drawbacks of MOOCs are related to the lack of motivation from the student, instructor, or the university which provides little or no support, MOOCs present real challenges for teaching students online. As institutions and instructors work to overcome the challenges of offering MOOCs, one participant reminds the researchers in this study that first, everyone must be able to define and understand MOOCs. While question branching logic was used in the survey to ascertain whether participants were aware of MOOCs, this participant stated,

> You have a flaw in your survey. In the introduction, you discuss MOOCs under the assumption that the people you desire to respond to this survey will understand the meaning. Unfortunately, at [university], we do not use this term; therefore, we do not understand the meaning (definition) of the term. You need to ensure you provide all appropriate information to ensure respondent understanding… do not assume they will know. In summary, if institutions, instructors or students are unaware of MOOCs; they will never be able to fully obtain the benefits which come from offering MOOCs.

The Challenges of Offering MOOCs

When asked specifically about the challenges of offering MOOCs at their institutions, participants discussed the issues or concerns pertaining to faculty, institutional leadership and resources, academics, and students. This section of the findings will focus on the perceived challenges of offering MOOCs.

Faculty Issues and Concerns

Participants expressed concerns with faculty's acceptance of, skill in developing, and time management of MOOCs. Participants also discussed the class size and teaching load associated with facilitating MOOCs. However, the majority of participants discussed the loss of traditional class face-to-face interaction as their biggest concern. One participant expressed the following, "the real-life interaction between instructor and student and the relationships/networks built in traditional face-to-face classrooms provide educational benefits and life-skills that cannot be obtained in an online classroom".

While, other participants expressed the concern that colleagues may be unwilling to learn or mistrust new technology. The unwillingness to learn or the mistrust of this "new" technology, as one participant stated is "the challenge [of] determining the content that can be delivered successfully…" or may be related the time management required to successfully teach a MOOCs course. One participant stated MOOCs are time-consuming and faculty are not trained to be web designers. Finally, participants discussed concerns about many faculty "are simply overloaded and will not have time to dedicate to a MOOC." or with the large number of students who may enroll in these courses.

Lack of Resources and Institutional Leadership Support

Participants are also concerned with the perceived lack or limited number of resources available to offer MOOCs in the forms of technology, IT support, and the possible lack of funding due to the high cost of MOOCs. The perceived limitation of technology at their institutions was also discussed in relation to the lack of institutional leadership support. A participant noted the "leadership of all levels seems stuck in the past regarding teaching and learning with technology". However the lack of leadership support for one participant was not the issue, the participant stated "the Provost is pushing for more online education, but the quality is poor and the interest from faculty is very low".

Academic Concerns

The lack of support from institutional leaders may be attributed to the same concerns faculty have with accreditation issues. Participants expressed that MOOCs may be better suited for professional development and not courses that require students to receive course credit or must meet the requirements for institutions to maintain their accreditation status. One participant summed up the concerns of the major challenges by stating "almost everything – accreditation, acceptance by disciplines, assessment, institutional support, [and] instructional support".

Lastly when discussing the challenges, participants expressed concerns related to the student who may enroll in MOOCs. Participants frequently mentioned the high dropout rates and most often the low completion rates. The concerns over students are repeated findings discussed on the benefits and are also found in the responses to the question about the reasons for low completion rates.

Reasons for Low Completion Rates

Overwhelming participants considered the reason for the low completion rates in MOOCs as the lack of motivation, accountability, dedication, and self-discipline of students. A student's lack of motivation to complete MOOCs, as one participant stated, "…may be explained by the fact that people receive no tangible consequences (i.e., rewards, punishment, etc.) for dropping out of a MOOC". Thus, one participant drew the conclusion that the lack of motivation may be linked to accountability as some students know when [they] walk away there is little accountability to finish, saying "the student is anonymous in a MOOC. Those who have a greater likelihood to start and complete a fitness class do so when they have to be accountable to someone. If you can drop out and no one knows; well no shame in that. There is peer pressure in a class not in a MOOC". Some participants also discussed the perceived lack of dedication and self-discipline students possess to complete these time intensive courses. However, one participant noted, "I don't see the completion rate as a problem for MOOCs...students sign up on a whim and change their mind before the class starts, the course sounds interesting but after the first few minutes/days, they find it boring or too difficult or sloppily designed or they don't "connect" with someone via the class and are less motivated to come back, etc. There are things an instructor/institution can do to retain some of those students, but unless the low retention rate leads to excess costs, I can't see how it matters".

No matter whether or not the low completion rates are due to individual student characteristics, some participants felt MOOCs themselves are the reason. Participants noted that the overall structure of MOOCs may contribute to low completion rates. The MOOC being offered could have a large class size, boring format, and no real educational value. The course may also be too demanding or difficult, time consuming, or lack the personal attention a student desires from the instructor. One participant noted "I think completion rates of MOOCs will remain low because many of the courses are difficult and don't count toward a degree". By examining faculty perspectives on MOOCs, the findings revealed the need to involve faculty in the design, delivery of, and decisions to offer MOOCs. In doing so, institutions may be able to increase the benefits for all, remove some of the challenges, and increase completion rates.

Discussion

The researchers of this study examined the responses of over 390 current faculty members in a well-known university system regarding their perceptions of the benefits of MOOCs. Some respondents also included unsolicited drawbacks associated with MOOCs. The study's results were not only consistent with the growing literature base, but also offered insight as to areas of needed professional development for faculty members and future research especially by human resource development scholars and practitioners engaged in virtual learning research and training. Through systematic data analysis, two over-arching perceptions of MOOC benefits emerged: benefits to students and benefits to the sponsoring institution and programs within the institutions.

A rich base of literature exists outlining the benefits of MOOCs for students (Rodriguez, 2012; Becker, 2013; Mallon, 2013). In this study, faculty members noted students value the accessibility to high quality resources and education, otherwise unavailable at the local university or perhaps in their entire country. This powerful benefit was also noted in a study by Tamburri (2014). The peda-gogical application of synchronous and asynchronous digital tools creates a rich personal learning community for students in institutions of higher learning. In the case of industry where HRD practitioners provide training and continuing professional education, MOOCs should be of great benefit to both trainees and trainers. In the case of cMOOCs, as students connect with other learners, and engage in learning together, they become vested in the knowledge creation process. They work to sustain the established learning network and gain new perspectives from their peers. Kahu (2014) noted that when students become vested in this manner, they exponentially improve their understanding of the content being learned.

Flexibility of class time was another benefit faculty members emphasized. MOOCs allow the students to participate in learning experiences at the time of day they learn best, therefore they begin the course automatically self-regulating their learning experiences. As with other online course environments, time management and organizational abilities are required for successful participation in a MOOC. As students determine when they participate in the MOOC, these skills will continually improve the students' optimal learning threshold. Jensen's (2005) work supports these noted benefits of class time flexibility.

The self-paced, no grade-pressure nature of a MOOC may be especially appealing for many students, as noted by faculty members in this study. Unlike a traditional online course, these courses may be offered at no financial expense to the student. Another unique feature of the MOOC, its 'openness,' allows students different types of learning opportunities. Students can participate in the full course for credit, audit the course with no intention of completing assignments for credit (Kizilcec, Piech, & Schneider, 2013), or engage in only a targeted area to gain knowledge about a particular topic (Mallon, 2013; Wang & Baker, 2014). These options of enrolling in a MOOC with no intention of completing the full course for credit may contribute to the concern of low MOOC completion rates. The novel student participation features associated with MOOCs challenge the traditional view of course persistence rates, resulting in completion rate data that may not be an accurate measure of a course's effectiveness.

As noted by Clow (2013) MOOCs have higher dropout rates when compared to traditional face-to-face courses. Thus, only about 10% of the learners who enroll in MOOCs successfully complete the course (Daniel, 2012; Sandeen, 2013).

The study's other noted broad benefit of MOOCs can be defined as the advantage to the institution or program offering the MOOC. Due to the nature of a MOOC, it can reach audiences worldwide. The MOOC, dependent on its effectiveness, can popularize both the institution, as well as the instructor, which may serve as a recruitment tool for perspective students as it was the case with San Jose State University in California (Young, 2013).

In addition to reaching a broad audience, other institutional benefits include the direct impact on course quality as well as professional development opportunities. As MOOCs are unique in their structure and purpose, instructors need to determine which courses should be offered in a MOOC format, the related pedagogical issues, and the cognitive accessibility and instructional design of the course (Clara & Barbera, 2013).

Within this study, one of the most poignant comments from faculty members regarded the lack of familiarity with MOOCs. Although MOOCs are well established in many sectors of higher education (McCully, 2012), it cannot be presumed that all institutions or faculty members have experience or knowledge regarding MOOCs. This leads to questions of institution adoption and support. Faculty members clearly need professional development opportunities to explore the potential application of MOOCs in their specific field of study.

Although many of the study's findings are corroborated by the literature, this study raised questions regarding faculty members' perceptions of the overall purpose, design, adoption, pedagogy, and implementation of MOOCs. It is anticipated this paper will be one of a series exploring the issues of incorporating and offering MOOCs within an established university system in a well-known and respected university in southern United States.

References

Allen, I. E., & Seaman, J. (2013). *Changing course: Ten years of tracking online education in the United States.* Babson Park, MA: Babson Survey Research Group and Quahog Research Group. http://www.onlinelearningsurvey.com/reports/changingcourse.pdf.

Anderson, T. & Dron, J. (2012). Learning technology through three generations of technology enhanced distance education pedagogy. *Revisia Mexicana de Bachillerato a Distancia*, 1-14. http://www.eurodl.org/materials/contrib/2012/Anderson_Dron.pdf

Anderson, T., & Kanuka, H. (1997). On-line forums: New platforms for professional development and group collaboration. *Journal of Computer-Mediated Communication, 3*(3), [online]. Available: http://onlinelibrary.wiley.com/doi/10.1111/j.1083-6101.1997.tb00078.x/full.

Becker, B. W. (2013). Connecting MOOCs and library services. *Behavioral & Social Sciences Librarian, 32*(2), 135-138.

Bonk, C. J. (2002). *Online training in an online world.* Bloomington, IN: CourseShare.com.

Carey, K., (2013). Obama, Rubio agree on one thing: Technology could fix the higher ed mess. Slate Magazine Online, http://www.

slate.com/blogs/future_tense/2013/02/13/state_of_the_union_moocs_obama_rubio_agree_on_using_tech_to_fix_higher_ed.html.

Clark, B. R. (1998). *Creating entrepreneurial universities: Organizational pathways of transformations.* Oxford, England: Pergamon for the IAU Press: 131-132.

Clara, M., & Barbera, E. (2013). Learning online: Massive Open Online Courses (MOOCs), connectivism, and cultural psychology. *Distance Education, 34*(1), 129-136.

Clow, D. (2013). MOOCs and the funnel of participation. In *Proceedings of the Third International Conference on Learning Analytics and Knowledge* (pp. 185-189). ACM, New York.

Cull, S., Reed, D. & Kirk, K. (2010). *Student motivation and engagement in online courses.* Teaching Geoscience Online - A Workshop for Digital Faculty. Retrieved at: http://serc.carleton.edu/NAGTWorkshops/online/motivation.html.

Daniel, J. (2012). Making sense of MOOCs: Musing in a maze of myth, paradox and possibility. *Journal of interactive Media in education, 2012*(3). Retrieved from http://jime.open.ac.uk/articles/10.5334/2012-18/ .

Dillman, D.A. (2000). *Mail and internet surveys: The tailored design method.* New York: Wiley.

Hachey, A.C., Wladis, C.W., & Conway, K.M. (2012). Is the second time the charm? Investigating trends in online enrollment, retention and success. *The Journal of Educators Online, 9*(1).

Jensen, E. (2005). *Teaching with the brain in mind* (2nd ed). Alexandria, VA: ASCD.

Jordan, K. (2013). Initial trends in enrollment and completion of massive open online courses. *International Review of Research in Open and Distance Learning 15*(1), 133-160.

Kahu, E. (n.d). Framing student engagement in higher education. *Studies in Higher Education, 38*(5), 758- 773.

Ke, J. (2011). Professional perceptions of the effectiveness of online versus face-to-face continuing professional education courses. Unpublished dissertation, Texas A&M University. Retrieved from http://repository.tamu.edu/handle/1969.1/ETD-TAMU-2010-08-8518

Kizilcec, R.F., Piech, C., & Schneider, E. (2013). *Deconstructing disengagement: Analyzing learner subpopulations in massive open online courses.* Paper presented at the Third International Conference on Learning Analytics and Knowledge, 4-8-2013 (pp. 170-179). ACM.

Koutropoulos, A., & Hougue, R.J. (2012). How to succeed in a MOOC - Massive Open Online Course. *Learning Solutions Magazine, 1*(5).

Leckart, S. (2012). *The Stanford education experiment could change higher education forever.* Wired Magazine. Retrieved from http://www.wired.com/wiredscience/2012/03/ff_aiclass/3/.

Mallon, M. (2013). MOOCs. *Public Services Quarterly, 9*(1), 46-53.

Meyer, R. (2012). What it's like to teach a MOOC and what the heck's a MOOC?

Retrieved from: http://www.theatlantic.com/technology/archive/2012/07/what-its-like-to-teach-a-mooc-and-what-the-hecks-a-mooc/260000/.

McCully, G. (2012). "University Unbound" Rebounds: Can MOOCs "Educate" as Well as Train? *New England Journal of Higher Education*.

Miller, M. D. (2014). *Minds online: Teaching effectively with technology*. Cambridge, Massachusetts: Harvard University Press.

Nafukho, F. M., & Muyia, M.A. H. (2014). Entrepreneurial leadership and transformation of universities in Africa. In F. M. Nafukho, M.A.H. Muyia & Irby, B. J. (Eds.). *Governance and transformation of universities in Africa*. Charlotte, NC: Information Age Publishing.

Nafukho F. M, & Wawire N. H. W. (2004). *Developing entrepreneurial universities in Africa*. In C. Momanyi, C. & N. H. W. Wawire (eds.). Disparities in Science, Technology, Environment, HIV/AIDS and Education (pp. 196-203). Nairobi: Association of Third World Studies.

Newman, M. (2013). Credit where credit is due in non-credit adult education. *Concept*, 4(2), 1-20.

November, A. (2010). *Empowering students with technology (2nd ed)*. Thousand Oaks, CA: Corwin.

Oxford Dictionaries (2014). Oxford University Press. Retrieved from http://www.oxforddictionaries.com/definition/english/MOOC?q=mooc.

Richardson, J. & Swan, K. (2003). Examining social presence in online courses in relation to students' perceived learning and satisfaction. *Journal of Asynchronous Learning Networks*, 7(1), 68-88.

Rodriguez, C. (2012). MOOCs and the AI-Stanford Like Courses: Two Successful and Distinct Course Formats for Massive Open Online Courses. *European Journal of Open, Distance and E-Learning*.

Sandeen, C. (2013). Assessment's place in the new MOOC world. *Research & Practice in Assessment*, 8(1), 5-12.

Scholz, C. W. (2013). MOOCs and the liberal arts college. *Journal of Online Learning and Teaching*, 9(2), 249-260.

Shirky, C. (2012, November 12). Napster, Udacity, and the academy [Web log post]. Retrieved from http://www.shirky.com/weblog/2012/11/napster-udacity-and-the-academy/.

Tamburri, R. (2014). An interview with Canadian MOOC pioneer George Siemens. Retrieved from: http://www.universityaffairs.ca/features/feature-article/an-interview-with-canadian-mooc-pioneer-george-siemens/.

Wang, Y. & Baker, R. (2014). MOOC learner motivation and course completion rates. *MOOC Research Initiative - Final Report*. Retrieved from http://www.moocresearch.com/wp-content/uploads/2014/06/MRI-Report-WangBaker-June-2014.pdf

Witt, P. L., Wheeless, L. R., & Allen, M. (2004). A meta-analytical review of the relationship between teacher immediacy and student learning. *Communication Monographs*, 71(2), 184-207.

Young, J. R. (2013). Learning from business. Retrieved from http://chronicle.com/article/Learning-From-Big-Business/138811/.

Yuan, L., Powell, S., & Cetis, J. (2013). MOOCs and open education: Implications for higher education. *Cetis White Paper.*

Ziderman, A., & Albrecht, D. (1995) *Financing universities in developing countries.* Washington, D.C.: The Falmer Press.

Definition of Terms

Massively Open Online Course (MOOC) – a course of study made freely available online to a large number of people.

Cognitive/behavioral learning theory – describes the role of cognition in determining and predicting the behavioral pattern of an individual. In other words, the way individuals think of themselves, their environment, and the future all impact the behavior they display.

Social constructivist learning theory – focuses on an individual's learning that takes place because of their interactions in a group.

Connectivist learning theory – the view that learning can reside outside of ourselves, is focused on connecting specialized information sets, and the connections that enable us to learn more are more important than our current state of knowing.

Personal Learning Network (PLN) – an informal learning network that consists of people a learner interacts with and derives knowledge from.
(video link: https://www.youtube.com/watch?t=11&v=hLLpWqp-owo)

xMOOC -- xMOOC -- A more traditionally organized post-secondary online course utilizing more familiar higher education teaching methods such as pre-recorded lectures, texts and quizzes, usually sponsored by universities or commercial entities and which may offer certificates and/or course credits.

cMOOC -- In a cMOOC environment the participants in the course act as both teachers and students, sharing information and engaging in a joint teaching and learning experience through intense interaction facilitated by technology.

Question branching logic – a survey research technique that displays only questions that are relevant to the participant based on previous answers.

The Intersection of Exemplar Professional Accreditation Standards and Quality Matters Rubric Standards for Best Practice in Distance Education

Nancy E. Krusen[A]

The process of accreditation is a systematic review through which the public may be assured that an institution provides quality education. Accrediting bodies typically address the quality of the program and institution, not course design. Distance education components may or may not be included in accreditation assessment. Quality MattersTM (QM) is a research-centered approach to continuous quality improvement for online learning. QM addresses only course design, not the quality of a program or institution. The primary aim of this article is to examine the intersection of exemplar accreditation standards from a representative professional association and Quality MattersTM Rubric Standards (QM Standards) for best practice in distance education. The author evaluated primary standards documents for congruity and disparity, strengths and limitations. Such close examination may serve as a model for accrediting bodies to engage in open dialog to improve the quality of distance education. The author concluded that standards are complementary in this instance; however, the numerous differences indicate opportunities for enhancement. The intent of each accrediting organization and their respective standards is the benefit of stakeholders. The author recommends collaboration between accreditation agencies and institutes of higher education to modify standards related to distance education. Modifications to each set of standards have the potential to improve the quality of distance education for the benefit of institutions of higher education, the public, learners, and their respective professions.

Keywords: accreditation, distance education

Introduction

The process of accreditation is a systematic review through which the public may be assured that an institution provides quality education. Accrediting bodies typically address the quality of the program and institution, not course design. Quality MattersTM (QM) is a research-centered approach to continuous quality improvement for online learning (https://www.qualitymatters.org/). Quality

---

[A] **Dr. Krusen** is an associate professor in the School of Occupational Therapy at Pacific University, Oregon, USA. Her research interests include teaching and learning, qualitative methods of research, and the constructs of the Occupational Adaptation theoretical frame of reference. She has received university grants for education and distance technology, community outreach, and international education. She has published papers in peer-reviewed journals and has a book chapter addressing aging and disability. Dr. Krusen lives primarily in Colorado, where she enjoys hiking, reading, snowshoeing, music performance, reverse carpentry, and cooking for an irregular parade of younglings.

doi: 10.18278/il.4.2.9

MattersTM addresses only course design, not the quality of a program or institution. The primary aim of this article is to examine the intersection of exemplar accreditation standards from a representative professional association and Quality MattersTM Rubric Standards (QM Standards) for best practice in distance education. Such close examination may serve as a model for accrediting bodies to engage in open dialog to improve the quality of distance education. This comparative exercise focuses on exemplar standards of the Accreditation Council for Occupational Therapy Education® (ACOTE) of the American Occupational Therapy Association (AOTA). The ACOTE standards are similar in format and intent to those of other health professions.

Accreditation in Higher Education

In the United States, accreditation is a process of voluntary, external, non-governmental, systematic review of educational institutions and programs for quality assurance and improvement (Eaton, 2009). Accreditation is intended to support improvement of the institution or program. The Council for Higher Education Accreditation (CHEA) is the largest non-governmental higher education organization in the United States, supporting academic quality through voluntary accreditation. The United States Department of Education (USDE) publishes a database of nationally recognized accrediting bodies determined to meet acceptable levels of quality for programs and degrees within institutions of higher education (http://ope.ed.gov/accreditation/). USDE does not accredit individual degrees, programs or institutions. CHEA focuses on academic quality in courses, programs, and degrees, while USDE focuses on financial and administrative practices for federal student aid funding. CHEA reports that more than 8,400 degree and non-degree-granting institutions are recognized as specialized accrediting organizations either through USDE, through CHEA or both (CHEA, 2014). These national, regional, and specialized accrediting bodies develop specific evaluation standards and guidelines used during peer review for determination of compliance. Many of these are health and human service professions such as audiology, nursing, optometry, and pharmacy. Accreditation directly benefits the public, students, institutions of higher education, and the professions overseen via specialized accrediting bodies such as ACOTE.

Accreditation Council for Occupational Therapy Education

ACOTE accredits educational program degree levels for the occupational therapist (OT) and the occupational therapy assistant (OT). USDE and CHEA each recognize ACOTE as an accrediting organization. ACOTE "establishes comprehensive standards for occupational therapy education at multiple degree levels, thereby supporting the preparation of competent occupational therapists and occupational therapy assistants" (AOTA, 2013 p3). The most current ACOTE Standards and Interpretive Guide, consistent with the requirement of the USDE, became effective July 31, 2013 (AOTA, 2013). The Standards are competency-based, describing the knowledge and skills necessary for occupational therapy practitioners to serve in a variety of roles in response to the "rapidly changing and dynamic nature of contemporary health and human services delivery systems" (ACOTE, 2011 p1). ACOTE does not address course design. ACOTE routinely collects data from educational programs, including the percentage of distance components. The latest data reporting current distance education components for entry-level OT doctoral degree programs, entry-level OT master's degree programs, and occupational therapy assistant programs are available here: (AOTA, 2014). ACOTE/AOTA categorize the raw data according to the USDE definition of distance education as that which uses "one or more of the following technologies to deliver instruction to students who are separated from the instructor and to support regular and substantive interaction between the students and the instructor, either synchronously or asynchronously. The technologies may include:

1. The Internet;
2. One-way and two-way transmissions through open broadcast, closed circuit, cable, microwave, broadband lines, fiber optics, satellite, or wireless communications devices;
3. Audio conferencing; or
4. Video cassettes, DVDs, and CD-ROMs, if the cassettes, DVDs, or CD-ROMs are used in a course in conjunction with any of the technologies listed in paragraphs (1) through (3)" (2014).

In an effort to determine quality associated with distance components, ACOTE publishes a Distance Education Checklist of 20 items addressing related 2006 Accreditation Standards, which program faculty and accreditation evaluators use to determine compliance (AOTA, 2006). Professional develop-ment is available to program directors and practitioners interested in serving as accreditation evaluators. No research currently addresses the role of ACOTE Standards in the quality of education.

Distance Education

Multiple and various definitions of distance education describe specific methods of delivery; note students as being separated from the instructor; and enumerate a variety of types of interaction, including the Internet, audio-conference, video-conference, synchronous and asynchronous chat, DVD, CD-ROM, etc. For the purpose of this article, the author adopts the CHEA definition of distance education, "application of electronic technology to teaching and learning" (Eaton, 2001, p. 3). CHEA has historically been instrumental in publishing documents describing the fundamental components for accreditation to address distance education. For example, the CHEA "Fact Sheet #2: The role of accreditation and assuring quality in electronically delivered distance education 2001" describes the role of accreditation in assuring quality, as well as the ways in which national and regional accrediting agencies manage standards and accountability for distance education (CHEA, 2001).

Changes in distance education present new challenges for accrediting bodies (Legon, 2006). Regional and national accrediting agencies are now responsible to examine distance education in their routine review of programs and institutions of higher education. Since 2010, the USDE has required each institution under review to "demonstrate its evaluation of distance education and/or correspondence education in order to retain distance education and/or correspondence education in its scope of recognition" (USDE, 2014). Keil and Brown (2014) reviewed six current regional and national accrediting organizations in the United States, examining policies addressing "institutional context and commitment; curriculum and instruction; faculty and faculty support; student support; and evaluation and assessment" (p. 1). Quality and best practice in education are repeated concerns across each agency and each policy area.

Quality Matters

Before the QM Standards were developed, several regional accrediting bodies studied distance education, expressing the need to develop a means for relevant measurement to assure quality. The Higher Education Opportunity Act (Act) established requisites for accrediting bodies to assure the quality of programs offered through distance education (Higher Education Opportunity Act of 2008, Pub. L. No. 110–315, 122 Stat. 3494 (2008)). Further, the Act requires that the agency or association's standards "effectively address the quality of an institution's distance education" but "shall not be required to have separate standards, procedures, or policies for the evaluation of distance education" (Higher Education Opportunity Act of 2008, Pub. L. No. 110–315, 122 Stat. 3325 (2008)).

In 2003, the MarylandOnline (MOL) Consortium initiated the Quality Matters project. MOL is a voluntary, non-profit group of post-secondary educational institutions in the state of Maryland. The QM project proposed the creation of standards for course design and peer review, assuring the quality of online courses. QM does not address the quality of the program or institution. The USDE supported the project through the Fund for the Improvement of Postsecondary Education (FIPSE). The FIPSE grant supported the first finalized QM Rubric Standards, a process of course review, and an instructor worksheet. Developers created benchmark criteria for course assessment to be points of reference for best practice rather than rigid measures.

The current QM Standards (https://www.qualitymatters.org/), now in the fifth edition, are used to evaluate individual (blended or online) courses using 43 criteria categorized into eight general standards, listed below. QM Standards include detailed descriptions for each criterion for interpretation and implementation during course development and review. Each general standard contains an overview statement, relating its place in the process. Each specific Standard contains detailed annotations with explanation, instructions for interpretation, examples, and recommendations for application to blended courses.

1. Course Overview and Introduction
2. Learning Objectives (Competencies)
3. Assessment and Measurement
4. Instructional Materials
5. Course Activities and Learner Interaction
6. Course Technology
7. Learner Support
8. Accessibility and Usability

The QM program reflects a grass-roots heritage in which faculty experts collaborate, modifying the Standards for course design as distance education develops. In addition to course assessment, the broad goals of the QM program include faculty development and continuous improvement through critical analysis for the purpose of increased student engagement, learning, and satisfaction. QM also provides professional development to instructional designers, all levels of faculty, and academic administrators. Shattuck, Zimmerman and Adair (2014) describe the process of regular review of the QM Standards to ensure their applicability within a broad variety of educational levels and disciplines. They discuss the process of continuous improvement in relationship to Boyer's model of scholarship. QM is now a self-sustaining program and process for which institutions provide a fee-for-service or subscription to participate in professional development, including peer reviewer training to promote best practice in distance education.

Comparison and Analysis

Proliferation of distance education programs presents challenges for national, regional, and specialized degree granting organizations. The author evaluated primary standards documents from ACOTE and QM for congruity and disparity, strengths and limitations. For clarification, national, regional, and specialized accreditation are concerned with programs and institutions as a whole. Accreditation reviewers examine administrative concerns such as sponsorship of the institution, academic and student resources, fiscal management, operational and admission policies, strategic planning, and program evaluation. Reviewers may also examine curricular frameworks and content, particularly for specialized degrees and programs, however, QM reviewers assess and recognize only individual courses, without examination of larger institutional concerns. QM reviewers may see elements of institutional or programmatic, admin-istrative concerns addressed within a single course, but QM is not intended to be a substitute for the larger focus of national, regional or specialized accreditation (Legon, 2006).

The following table is a comparison between the ACOTE Standards on the Distance Education Checklist and the corresponding QM Standards. Many of the ACOTE Standards address institutional accreditation and cannot be assessed against the QM Standards focus at an individual course level. The comparison is an attempt to determine congruity, gaps, and opportunities. **The QM Standards Rubric may be reprinted only with** explicit permission of a QM staff member, which was not provided for this article. The QM **Higher Education Rubric, Fifth Edition, 2014 Standards only** are a**vailable for individual**, single-use **at the QM website**: https://www.qualitymatters.org/rubric. The downloadable document is intended solely for transparency to the public; the complete document with its rich explanations and supporting materials is available through paid services. The reader may contact MarylandOnline, Inc. at info@qualitymatters.org for information or reprint permission. ACOTE Standards are available for download at http://www.aota.org/-/media/Corporate/Files/EducationCareers/Accredit/Standards/2011-Standards-and-Interpretive-Guide-August-2013.pdf. ACOTE Distance Education Checklist, a portion of the ACOTE Standards, is available for download at http://www.aota.org/Education-Careers/Accreditation.aspx. The author, a long time ACOTE accreditation reviewer, updated the existing ACOTE Distance Education Checklist to reflect the corresponding 2011 Standards, effective July 31, 2013. The first column within the table lists the ACOTE Standard. The second column lists recommended ACOTE questions to illuminate each Standard. The third column lists the related QM Standard, noted as *essential* where relevant. The last column contains the author's comments about the relationship between the two sets of standards.

Table 1

Comparison of Distance Education Checklist ACOTE Standards with Quality Matters Standards Rubric

ACOTE Standard	ACOTE Clarifying Question	QM Standard	Commentary
General Admission/ Policies/Publications			
Standard A.3.1. Admission of students to the occupational therapy / therapy assistant program must be made in accordance with the practices of the institution. There must be stated admission criteria that are clearly defined and published and reflective of the demands of the program.	Do the stated admission criteria inform students of technology and other requirements for the distance education components of the program?	Standard 1.5 Pertains to technology requirements.	Close match. Institutional practices and QM technological course requirements.
Standard A.3.3. Policies pertaining to standards for admission, advanced placement, transfer of credit, credit for experiential learning (if applicable), and prerequisite educational or work experience requirements must be readily accessible to prospective students and the public.	Are students informed about required competencies for the distance education component?	Standard 1.6 Pertains to prerequisite knowledge Standard 1.7 Pertains to technical skills	Close match. Institution and course identify prerequisite competencies for the discipline and for the use of course technology.
Standard A.4.1. All program publications and advertising – including, but not limited to, academic calendars, announcements, catalogs, handbooks, and Web sites – must accurately reflect the program offered.	Does advertising about the program clearly and accurately represent the distance/electronic component of the curriculum? Are students informed about the component of distance learning?	Standard 1.1 (Essential) Pertains to course navigation	Limited match. Institution or program indicates which courses or program elements may include distance learning. QM indicates what to expect for the course, including where components may be found.
Faculty Services			
Standard A.2.6. The program director and faculty must possess the academic qualifications and backgrounds (identified in documented descriptions of roles and responsibilities) that are necessary to meet program objectives and the mission of the institution.	Do the faculty in the program offering distance education have experience with a distance/ electronic learning format?	Not addressed	No match. Recognized QM courses may suggest the qualifications of faculty.

Standard A.2.11. *The faculty must have documented expertise in their area(s) of teaching responsibility and knowledge of the content delivery method (e.g., distance learning).*	Do faculty using the distance/electronic learning format have the necessary expertise to ensure appropriate content delivery?	*Not addressed*	No match. Recognized QM courses may suggest the expertise of faculty.
Standard A.5.2. *The program director and each faculty member who teaches two or more courses must have a current written professional growth and development plan. Each plan must contain the signature of the faculty member and supervisor. At a minimum, the plan must include, but need not be limited to,* *· Goals to enhance the faculty member's ability to fulfill designated responsibilities (e.g., goals related to currency in areas of teaching responsibility, teaching effectiveness, research, scholarly activity).* *· Specific measurable action steps with expected timelines by which the faculty member will achieve the goals.* *· Evidence of annual updates of action steps and goals as they are met or as circumstances change.* *· Identification of the ways in which the faculty member's professional development plan will contribute to attaining the program's strategic goals.*	Are distance/electronic learning objectives included in professional development plans of faculty responsible for this type of content delivery?	*Not addressed*	No match. Completed QM professional development may suggest scholarship of faculty.
Budget			
Standard A.2.17. *The program must be allocated a budget of regular institutional funds, not including grants, gifts, and other restricted sources, sufficient to implement and maintain the objectives of the program and to fulfill the program's obligation to matriculated and entering students.*	Is the organizational structure of distance education reflected in the overall budget?	*Not addressed*	Adoption of the QM rubric or institutional membership may indicate fiscal planning including course quality.
	Are funds available for faculty to learn distance/electronic learning format?	*Not addressed*	
	Is adequate support available for faculty preparing courses offered electronically?	*Not addressed*	
	Is the budget sufficient for updating technology?	*Not addressed*	

Student Services			
Standard A.2.18. Classroom and laboratories must be provided that are consistent with the program's educational objectives, teaching methods, number of students, and safety and health standards of the institution, and must allow for efficient operation of the program.	Are classrooms, labs, technology, and resources adequate to support a distance learning environment education?	*Standard 6.1 (Essential) Pertains to course tools Standard 7.1 (Essential) Pertains to course instructions*	Close match. Institution and QM verify technology and support provided. Indicate whether instructor is directing student to resources. Both related to objectives. QM addresses materials and methods in sections 4 & 5.
Standard A.2.19. If the program offers distance education, it must include · A process through which the program establishes that the student who registers in a distance education course or program is the same student who participates in and completes the program and receives academic credit, · *Technology and resources that are adequate to support a distance-learning environment, and* · *A process to ensure that faculty are adequately trained and skilled to use distance education methodologies.*	Does the program have a process through which it establishes that the student who registers in a distance education course or program is the same student who participates in and completes the program and receives the academic credit?	*Not addressed* *Standard 6.3 (Essential) Pertains to technology Standard 6.4 Pertains to technology*	QM course review could be expanded to address security in testing or assignment submission. Close match. Institution and QM describe relevant technologic tools, readily available, downloadable, cost-effective. Adoption of the QM rubric or institutional membership may indicate commitment to professional development.
Standard A.2.26. Students must have ready access to a supply of current and relevant books, journals, periodicals, computers, software, and other reference materials needed for the practice areas and to meet the requirements of the curriculum. This may include, but is not limited to, libraries, online services, interlibrary loan, and resource centers.	Are related materials readily available? Are they sufficient for use with distance/electronic learning format? Is the help desk readily available when course most likely accessed? Is training available for students?	*Standard 7.3 Pertains to academic support Standard 7.4 Pertains to student services*	Close match. Institutional and QM direct links to resources and student services; library, financial, health, technology.
Curriculum and instruction			

Curriculum and instruction			
Standard A.6.7. The curriculum design must reflect the mission and philosophy of both the occupational therapy program and the institution and must provide the basis for program planning, implementation, and evaluation. The design must identify curricular threads and educational goals and describe the selection of the content, scope, and sequencing of coursework.	Does the distance/ electronic learning format fit within the current curriculum design?	*Standard 2.2 (Essential) Pertains to learning objectives*	Limited match. QM addresses course level only consistency between module and course learning objectives. QM does not address curriculum design or relationship to mission.
Doctoral Standard A.6.8. The program must have clearly documented assessment measures by which students are regularly evaluated on their acquisition of knowledge, skills, attitudes, and competencies required for graduation.	Are students evaluated on their acquisition of knowledge, skills, attitudes, and competencies? Are the assignments available through electronic learning appropriate for the development of competencies?	*Standard 3.1 (Essential) Pertains to assessments Standard 3.5 Pertains to self-assessment*	Limited match. Institution and QM document consistency of course goals, learning objectives, and assessment with single course. QM does not align course with larger programmatic or degree competencies.
Standard A.6.9. The program must have written syllabi for each course that include course objectives and learning activities that, in total, reflect all course content required by the Standards. Instructional methods (e.g., presentations, demonstrations, discussion) and materials used to accomplish course objectives must be documented. Programs must also demonstrate the consistency between course syllabi and the curriculum design.	Are the syllabi clear and easy to understand with no opportunities for alternate interpretation of content? Are the learning objectives and competencies appropriate in rigor and breadth of non-distance courses?	*Standard 1.2 (Essential) Pertains to course syllabus Standard 2.1 (Essential) Pertains to measurable outcomes Standard 2.4 (Essential) Pertains to course activities Standard 5.1 (Essential) Pertains to course activities Standard 5.2 (Essential) Pertains to active learning*	Limited match. Institutional template and QM require clarity in syllabus. QM does not address consistency between course syllabus and curriculum design.
Evaluation and assessment			
Standard A.3.6. Evaluation content and methods must be consistent with the curriculum design, objectives, and competencies of the didactic, fieldwork, and experiential components of the program.	Is evaluation/assessment of student performance consistent? Are technologies available for instructor/student interaction (e.g., e-mail, chat rooms, fax, threaded discussions, phone)?	*Standard 3.2 (Essential) Pertains to grading policy Standard 3.3 (Essential) Pertains to evaluation criteria Standard 3.4 Pertains to assessment instruments*	Close match. Institution and QM require clarity in means of assessment, grading criteria, and feedback for individual courses. QM does not address curriculum design.

	Does the distance education portion of the program result in outcomes of the same quality as other on-site courses?		
Standard A.3.7. Evaluation must be conducted on a regular basis to provide students and program officials with timely indications of the students' progress and academic standing.	Is there timely instructor response/feedback to student assignments and inquiry?	*Standard 3.5 Pertains to self-assessment Standard 5.3 Pertains to instructor response*	Close match. Institutional and QM concern for timely feedback. QM indicators for multiple opportunities to track progress with timely feedback support transparency in student assessment.
Standard A.5.3. Programs must routinely secure and document sufficient qualitative and quantitative information to allow for meaningful analysis about the extent to which the program is meeting its stated goals and objectives. This must include, but need not be limited to • *Faculty effectiveness in their assigned teaching responsibilities.* • *Students' progression through the program.* • *Fieldwork and experiential component performance evaluation.* • *Student evaluation of fieldwork and the experiential component experience.* • *Student satisfaction with the program.* • *Graduates' performance on the NBCOT certification exam.* • *Graduates' job placement and performance based on employer satisfaction.* • *Graduates' scholarly activity (e.g., presentations, publications, grants obtained, state and national leadership positions, awards).*	Is there an appropriate means of evaluating faculty effectiveness in delivery of distance education components?	*Not addressed*	Adoption of the QM rubric or institutional membership may indicate commitment to an examination of faculty effectiveness. QM course review could be expanded to address course and faculty evaluation.

Standard A.5.5. The results of ongoing evaluation must be appropriately reflected in the program's strategic plan, curriculum, and other dimensions of the program.	Are there examples of how evaluation results have been reflected in curriculum changes, strategic plan, etc.?	Not addressed	Program evaluation and strategic planning is currently beyond the scope of QM. Adoption of the QM rubric or institutional membership may indicate incorporation of data into program evaluation.
Standard A.6.8. The program must have clearly documented assessment measures by which students are regularly evaluated on their acquisition of knowledge, skills, attitudes, and competencies required for graduation.	How have the usual methods of measuring communication, comprehension, synthesis, etc. been adapted to assess electronically offered courses? Are technologies available for instructor/student and student/student interaction (e.g., e-mail, chat rooms, fax, threaded discussions, phone)?	Standard 3.5 Pertains to self-assessment Standard 6.1 (Essential) Pertains to course tools Standard 6.2 (Essential) Pertains to course tools	Close match. Institutional and QM concern for regular evaluation. QM supports learning objectives and competencies at the course level, with technologic tools for interaction.

2014 © QM Rubric paraphrased by Nancy E. Krusen
Related Standards from Distance Education Checklist 2006 ACOTE Standards converted to 2011 ACOTE Standards for Doctoral/Master's/OTA

Comparison of ACOTE Standards with QM Standards confirms the unique nature of each process. There are areas of close congruity, areas of limited congruity, and areas of incongruity across standards. There is congruity regarding admission policies, publications, and student services. Both sets of standards examine technology and support provided with instructor directions to student resources. There is congruity for evaluation and assessment. Both sets of standards recommend clarity in tracking student progress, identifying means of assessment, identifying grading criteria, and providing feedback to students within individual courses. There is limited congruity regarding finances, curriculum and instruction. Institutional standards explicitly address the area of budget. The consumer may imply budgetary support of distance education when institutions voluntarily subscribe to Quality Matters. Institutional and QM standards each examine minimal consistency between course goals, learning objectives, and assessment. There is poor congruity addressing faculty expertise or professional development. Though QM as an organization is devoted to development of faculty expertise, the standards rubric for course evaluation does not determine such qualifications. Institutional membership or individually recognized courses or faculty completion of QM peer review training may indicate faculty expertise. There are no areas of congruity for larger issues of curricular design, programmatic or degree competencies. While QM addresses consistency of course goals, learning objectives, and assessment within the syllabus of a single course, there are no connections to larger issues of curricular design, programmatic or degree competencies. Program evaluation and strategic planning are outside the scope of QM.

Implications/Recommendations

The comparison indicates instances of close, limited, and poor congruity across standards that address institutional practices and those which address individual course requirements. The comparison suggests opportunities for dialog between organizational members to consider modifications for increased congruence between institutional practices and individual course requirements. Keen opportunities exist in the areas of course design to align with curricular framework, and program evaluation for strategic planning. Such close examination may serve as a model for other professional accrediting bodies to engage in open dialog. Limited communication and lack of research across accrediting bodies perpetuates a fragmented system. The comparison of standards in this article suggests possibilities for complimentary cohesion without duplication. Could specialized professional accrediting bodies, such as ACOTE, examine course design as part of accreditation? ACOTE Standards appear to be missing items QM identifies as essential components of good quality distance education, particularly the design of learning objectives, instructional materials, and issues of accessibility and usability. Modifications to ACOTE Standards could include elements of course overview, learner-centered objectives, instructional materials and methods, course activities, and accessibility. Could QM examine the connection between individual courses and larger curricular concerns? QM Standards do not integrate individual courses with overall programmatic concerns, a vital part of professional education. Modifications to QM standards could include the alignment of individual course goals and learning objectives with programmatic mission, vision, and curricular design, demonstrating consistency across individual courses in support of professional programs and degrees.

Modifying standards within professional accrediting bodies and QM, and across other accrediting organizations has utility for education, practice and research. Careful writing could incorporate the missing concepts into updated standards documents for each respective organization without being prescriptive. Not all faculties who have background in a content area also have expertise in teaching. Faculty development to acquire expertise in distance education may enable improved clarity in course design reflective of institutional requirements, degree competencies, and overall program cohesion. Clear course design with program alignment is part of best practices to improve student engagement, satisfaction, and success (Ralston-Berg, 2014). Future research could include five "components" of teaching: (a) instructional design, (b) instructional delivery, (c) instructional assessment, (d) content expertise, and (e) course management (Arreola, 2000 p24). Researching our teaching, referred to as the Scholarship of Teaching and Learning (SoTL), could address many areas revealed in this study examining the influence of accreditation on learning. This author concurs with Keil and Brown (2014) that accreditation agencies and institutes of higher education could collaborate to modify standards related to distance education. For example, topics and questions may include:

1. How does institutional membership, professional development or adoption of the QM rubric indicate organizational commitment to faculty qualifications as distance educators?
2. Does adoption of the QM rubric or institutional memberships indicate

fiscal management used to implement and maintain the goals of the institution or program.
3. What is the best use of data from QM course reviews for incorporation into strategic planning and outcome evaluation?
4. How does learner engagement in course design elements influence overall programmatic or degree competencies?

Each of these items may close the gap between the two types of standards, with utility for initial or re-accreditation of institutions and programs.

Conclusion

The author concludes that exemplar ACOTE and QM Standards are generally well matched, with an excellent opportunity for mutual benefit. This conclusion reinforces that of Legon (2006). Legon notes consistency in his comparison of QM with accreditation standards for distance learning, also recommending further development of the QM Standards. As previously noted, specialized standards are concerned with general institutional compliance with operational and administrative matters that are outside the scope of QM reviews. QM Standards are specific to individual courses but do not address the linkages across curriculum design, competencies for graduation, or program evaluation, necessary components of professional education. Accrediting bodies for professional programs, such as ACOTE, typically address the quality of the program and institution, needing to add course design to their assessment. Together, the Standards are complementary. The intent of each accrediting organization and their respective standards is the benefit of stakeholders. Key points to the article are:

- Individual course design and structure cannot be examined in isolation from curricula, programs, degrees, or organizations for professional education.
- Individual course design and structure should be integral to programs for professional accreditation.
- Integration across accrediting body standards and quality improvement standards will promote best practice for distance education.

Revisions to each set of Standards have the potential to improve the quality of distance education. Modifications would benefit the public, students, institutions of higher education, and their respective professions. The author recommends additional research and collaboration to examine specific concerns of accreditation for distance education.

Key Points:
- **Individual course design and structure cannot be examined in isolation from curricula, programs, degrees, or organizations for professional education.**
- **Individual course design and structure should be integral to programs for professional accreditation.**
- **Integration across accrediting body standards and quality improvement standards will promote best practice for distance education.**

References

American Occupational Therapy Association. (2006). Distance Education Checklist 2006 ACOTE Standards. Retrieved from http://www.aota.org/education-careers/accreditation.aspx

American Occupational Therapy Association (2011). 2011 Accreditation Council for Occupational Therapy Education (ACOTE®) Standards and Interpretive Guide. Retrieved from http://www.aota.org/-/media/Corporate/Files/EducationCareers/Accredit/Standards/2011-Standards-and-Interpretive-Guide-August-2013.pdf

American Occupational Therapy Association (2013). Accreditation Council for Occupational Therapy Education Accreditation Manual, I. Introduction, p3. Retrieved from http://www.aota.org/-/media/Corporate/Files/EducationCareers/Accredit/Policies/47631/I%20Introduction.pdf

American Occupational Therapy Association. (2014, August 15). *Distance Education Entry-Level Occupational Therapy (OT) Educational Programs.* Retrieved from http://www.aota.org/-/media/Corporate/Files/EducationCareers/Schools/DistanceEd/anceEducationTopPercentageOT2013-2014.pdf

Arreola, R. (2000). *Developing a comprehensive faculty evaluation system: A handbook for college faculty and administrators on designing and operating a comprehensive faculty evaluation system, 2nd Ed.*, Boulton, MA: Anker Publishing.

Council for Higher Education Accreditation. (2014). *Database of institutions and programs accredited by recognized United States accrediting organizations.* [Data file]. Retrieved from http://www.chea.org/search/

Council for Higher Education Accreditation. (2001). *Fact Sheet #2: The role of accreditation and assuring quality in electronically delivered distance education 2001.* CHEA Council for Higher Education Accreditation. Retrieved from http://www.chea.org/pdf/fact_sheet_2_dist_learn_02.pdf

Eaton, Judith S. (2001). *CHEA Monograph Series 2001, Number 1, Distance learning: Academic and political challenges for higher education accreditation.* CHEA Council for Higher Education Accreditation. p. 3. Retrieved from http://www.chea.org/research/distance-learning/chea_dis_learning.pdf

Eaton, Judith S. (2009). *An overview of U.S. accreditation.* Council for Higher Education Accreditation. Retrieved from http://www.chea.org/pdf/2009.06_overview_of_us_accreditation.pdf

Higher Education Opportunity Act of 2008, Pub. L. No. 110–315, 122 Stat. 3494 (2008).

Higher Education Opportunity Act of 2008, Pub. L. No. 110–315, 122 Stat. 3325 (2008)).

Keil, S. & Brown, A. (2014.) Distance education policy standards: A review of current regional and national accrediting organizations in the United States. *Online Journal of Distance Learning Administration, 17*(3), np. Retrieved from https://www.westga.edu/~distance/ojdla/fall173/keil_brown173.html

Legon, R. (2006). *Comparison of the Quality Matters rubric to accreditation standards for distance learning.* Baltimore, MD: Quality Matters. Retrieved from https://confluence.delhi.edu/download/

attachments/74055682/Comparison+of+the+Quality+Matters+Rubric+-+Summary.pdf

Quality Matters. (2014). *Quality Matters Rubric Standards Fifth Edition, 2014 with assigned point values.* MarylandOnline. Retrieved from https://www.qualitymatters.org/node/2305/download/QM%20Standards%20with%20Point%20Values%20Fifth%20Edition.pdf

Ralston-Berg, P. (2014). Surveying student perspectives of quality: Value of QM Rubric items. *Internet Learning Journal, 3*(1), 117-126.

Shattuck, K., Zimmerman, W.A., & Adair, D. (2014). Continuous improvement of the QM rubric and review processes: Scholarship of integration and application. *Internet Learning Journal, 3*(1), 25-34.

United States Department of Education. (2014, September 24). *Accreditation in the United States Guidelines for Petitions and Compliance Reports, Subpart A – General, 602.3.* Retrieved from http://www2.ed.gov/admins/finaid/accred/accreditation_pg12.html

United States Department of Education. (2014, September 24). *Accreditation in the United States Regional and National Institutional Accrediting Agencies.* Retrieved from http://www2.ed.gov/admins/finaid/accred/accreditation_pg6.html

Gamification Challenges and a Case Study in Online Learning

Darren Wilson,[A] Cynthia Calongne,[B] and Brook Henderson[C]

Two design models are introduced to feature the game-design elements and relationships that are critical for successful gamification. In online education, gamification employs game mechanics and incentives to encourage positive outcomes. Making good design decisions and offering a strong implementation are critical elements in the success of gamification. The study concludes by reviewing the results from a gamification case study and offers recommendations for future research.

Keywords: Social, analytics, knowledge, networks, visualization

---

[A] **Darren Wilson** is a researcher in gamification and is conducting dissertation research for a Doctor of Computer Science in Emerging Media at Colorado Technical University. He served as an Assistant Professor of Electrical and Computer Engineering at the US Air Force Academy from 2008-2011 and currently teaches high school physics, robotics, and statistics in Colorado Springs. His team won the 2005 Air Force Modeling and Simulation Award for Analysis.

[B] **Dr. Cynthia Calongne** is a researcher in virtual reality, game design and simulation. She joined Colorado Technical University's faculty as a Professor of Computer Science in 1996 and today teaches for CTU as an Adjunct Professor. Prior to teaching, she worked as a software engineer with Air Force Space Command. In 2010, her team won the $25,000 Grand Prize in the Federal Virtual World Challenge for The Mars Expedition Strategy Challenge.

[C] **Dr. S. Brook Henderson** worked for 15 years as a project manager for information technology. She was awarded the PMP (Project Management Professional) in 2002 by the Project Management Institute and is considered to be an expert on Project and Earned Value Management. Having achieved her doctorate in management with emphasis in organization development and project management from Colorado Technical University, she has left her former profession to join the faculty at American Public University System. Dr. Henderson has presented several papers at conferences and is a published author in her field. Most recently, in 2015, she is being included in a textbook for a review she wrote on Managing Complex Projects and Programs: How to Improve Leadership of Complex Initiatives Using a Third-Generation Approach by Richard Heaslip (2014) and a chapter on the History of Management Thought as well as two articles for a new book on global leadership set to be published in 2016. Brook lives in Colorado Springs, CO and can be reached on LinkedIn, Facebook, and email.

doi: 10.18278/il.4.2.10

Introduction

Gamification is not the same as a game. The educational use of gamification blends game-based mechanics (Schell, 2015) with an understanding of the needs, goals and values described by self-determination theory (Deci & Ryan, 2015) of intrinsic motivation. It encourages engagement and measurable benefits for online learning. Gamification is also part of the effort to address the needs of Generation Z, also known as "Gen Next" or "Gen I," including people born between the early 1990s and the early 2000s (Posnick-Goodwin, 2010). These folks have been thought of as smarter and more self-directed than other generations. They are able to process information more quickly than prior age groups, but they are not known for their ability to work in groups (Igel & Urguhort, 2012). The elements of mechanics and motivation merge to support applying game-based mechanics to existing educational courses to encourage engagement and measurable benefits for online learning. The authors of this study introduce the challenges associated with defining gamification and propose a model to support gamification design. The method and analysis sections review two case studies from earlier work in this field and conclude with recommendations for future research.

Theoretical Framework

Finding a succinct definition for gamification is a challenge. At its essence, is the notion that game-design elements, including game mechanics and game design principles, may transform an existing system into game-like constructs.

Gamification is not the same as a game. (Schell, 2015)

Examples of target systems include popular reward programs and academic course management tools. Definitions vary from this baseline as researchers relate the source of these game mechanics to video games, computer games or other game constructs. The centerpiece for this study is the search for an elusive definition, and to provide support for how researchers and professionals with little game design experience can leverage gamification through effective design and deployment to achieve predictable outcomes for students. During the course of the investigation mounted to find a common definition of gamification, certain themes emerged that offer great promise for advancing the research, as noted in Tables 1, 2 and 3.

Wilson (2015) proposes a model for mapping game-design elements to the values and beliefs of users and in turn, another model that examines their relationship to their perception of usefulness and task performance. The combination of bridging game mechanics with the values and task perceptions of the players helps to promote a game that fosters meaningful play (Huizinga, 1955; Salen, Tekinbas & Zimmerman, 2003). The result may lead to more applicable and predictable results for online education, engagement and learning.

Finding a succinct definition for gamification is a challenge.

The Quest for a Gamification Definition

Although gamification lacks a standard definition (Seaborn, 2015), common themes are found in the literature. For example, Denny (2013) defines gamification in terms of game elements used in non-game applications, whereas Li,

Table 1
Method descriptors from gamification definitions in peer-reviewed empirical studies

	Anderson (2013)	Bagley (2012)	Bista (2012a & 2012b)	Cafazzo (2012)	Cheong (2013)	Denny (2013)	Depura (2012)	Dominguez (2013)	Downes-Le Guin (2012)	Fitz-Walter (2011)	Fitz-Walter (2012)	Flatla (2011)	Foster (2012)	Frith (2012)	Cnaak (2012)	Goehle (2013)	Grant (2013)	Halcomen (2013)	Hamari (2013a)	Hamari (2013b)	Herr (2013)	Li (2012)	Lau (2011)	Massing (2013)	Passos (2011)	Smith (2012)	Thom (2012)	Witt (2011)
game design elements													x			x			x					x				
game elements			x	x		x											x											
game-inspired elements																											x	
computer-game elements	x																											
video-game elements		x							x											x								
video-game aspects								x																				
game features													x															
rewards/rewards systems				x																								
game mechanics					x		x									x								x	x			x
gameplay mechanics										x																		
video-game mechanics															x													
video-game techniques															x													
game dynamics		x									x																	
gamelike activities																										x		
game thinking									x							x				x								
game principles																											x	
game heuristics															x													
game patterns															x													
gameful-experience affordances																					x	x						

Grossman, and Fitzmaurice (2012) define it in terms of video-game elements used in non-game situations. Both studies employ a similar method in its definition (game elements vs. video-game elements) and a similar context (non-game applications vs. non-game situations). To explore these commonalities, the authors of this research study examined 47 peer-reviewed, empirical studies that were included in two meta-analyses (Seaborn 2015, Hamari, et al. 2014). Most of the 47 studies were obtained from the reference section of the meta-analyses using Google Scholar. Thirteen of the referenced studies were not available from Google Scholar and were retrieved electronically from the University of Colorado, Colorado Springs library computer system. Of these studies, 18 were excluded because they lacked a discernable definition of gamification. The definitional terms used in the remaining 29 articles were divided into three categories: method, context, and purpose.

> In this definition, the term *game design elements* (GDE) is not intended to describe a single method

Defining Gamification by Method

A matrix of the method descriptors used in the 29 papers is shown in Table 1. There is significant commonality in these methods, but this commonality becomes even more apparent when viewed through the lens of the gamification definition proposed by Deterding, Khaled, Nacke, and Dixon (2011, p. 2): "the use of game design elements in non-game contexts."

In this definition, the term game design elements (GDE) is not intended to describe a single method, as was Denny's *game elements*. Instead, it incorporates five distinct GDE levels to be applied in

Table 2
Mapping of method-based descriptors to GDE levels

GDE Levels	Method-based descriptors
Game interface design patterns	game elements, game-inspired elements, computer-game elements, video-game elements, game features, rewards/rewards systems, gamelike activities, gameful-experience affordances
Game design patterns and mechanics	game features, game dynamics, game patterns, gamelike activities, game principles, gameful-experience affordances
Game design principles and heuristics	game features, gameplay mechanics, video-game mechanics, game dynamics, gamelike activities, game principles, game patterns, gameful-experience affordances
Game models	game principles, game patterns, gameful-experience affordances
Game design methods	game thinking

the gamification process: game interface design patterns, game design patterns and mechanics, game design principles and heuristics, game models, and game design methods (Deterding, et al., 2011).

Each of the method descriptors included in Table 1 can be mapped to one or more of the GDE levels, as shown in Table 2. This mapping suggests that all of the method descriptors used in the 29 articles can be subsumed into the concept of GDE proposed in the Deterding, et al. (2011) definition.

Defining Gamification by Context

A similar analysis can be performed on the designated contexts for each of the definitions, which are listed in the upper portion of Table 3. With the possible exception of four of these contexts: web interactions, websites/software, solving problems, and the addressed product, each context is simply a rephrasing of the term *non-game contexts*, included in the Deterding, et al. definition (2011). Furthermore, it is arguable that the four possibly-excluded contexts, as used by their respective authors, also fall under the auspices of non-game contexts. This suggests that for definitions including only a method and a context, the Deterding, et al. (2011) definition is the de facto standard, as it is broad enough to include all—or nearly all—of the methods and contexts used.

Table 3

Context and purpose descriptors in gamification definitions from peer-reviewed, empirical studies

Descriptor	Anderson (2013)	Bagley (2012)	Bista (2012a & 2012b)	Cafazzo (2012)	Cheong (2013)	Denny (2013)	Depura (2012)	Dominguez (2013)	Downes-Le Guin (2012)	Fitz Walter (2011)	Fitz-Walter (2012)	Flatla (2011)	Foster (2012)	Frith (2012)	Gnauk (2012)	Goehle (2013)	Grant (2013)	Hakulinen (2013)	Hamari (2013a)	Hamari (2013b)	Hori (2013)	Li (2012)	Liu (2011)	Massung (2013)	Passos (2011)	Smith (2011)	Thom (2012)	Witt (2011)
non-game contexts										x			x					x	x		x			x				
non-game applications		x		x	x			x						x						x								
non-game educative contexts							x																					
non-game situations																						x						
non-game domains				x																								
other domains	x																											
other activities											x																	
outside of games																								x				
serious contexts																												x
unrelated to video games																	x											
web interactions			x																									
websites/software																									x			
solve problems								x							x													
addressed product														x														
motivate user	x									x																		
engage user/engagement		x	x						x	x	x							x	x	x		x						
affect user behavior				x								x																
user value creation																			x	x								
gamelike experience																			x	x								
enhance user experience	x													x							x							
increase user interest																x												

Defining Gamification by Purpose

Huotari and Hamari (2012), however, argue against the Deterding, et al. (2011) definition because it focuses on method instead of purpose. While purpose is a consistent aspect of gamification definitions—15 of the 29 studies included a purpose descriptor—their argument against method appears to be directed against the single method game elements, instead of the more comprehensive GDE.

A list of the purpose descriptors is shown in the lower portion of Table 3. All of these descriptors directly involve the user, either in prompting the user to act or in improving the user's experience with the gamified product. These are consistent with the importance of gameful experience and the user's value creation in Huotari and Hamari's (2012) definition and with Nicholson's (2012) user-centered framework.

While purpose is a consistent aspect of gamification definitions

A Model of Gamification Design

Any gamified system consists of three essential elements: a user, a non-game task for the user to perform, and a set of GDEs that motivate the user to perform the task. Combined, these form an element-based model of gamification, shown in *Figure 1*.

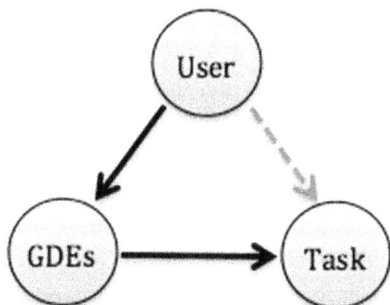

Figure 1. Element-based model of gamification

The non-game *task* in the model is used to represent a specific instance of a non-game context. The underlying goal of a gamified system is for the user to accomplish the task, illustrated by the dashed, gray arrow. Within any gamified system, GDEs are used to motivate the user to accomplish the task, illustrated by the two black arrows. Although the terminology differs slightly, this model is consistent with the Deterding, et al. (2011) definition: GDEs are used in a non-game task. Furthermore, the model adequately delineates two aspects of gamification's scope:

1. All gamified systems must have these three elements
2. Any non-game system with these three elements is a gamified system.

Although the elements in the above model are essential for any gamified system, *effective* gamification depends on the relationships between the elements, which are shown in *Figure 2*.

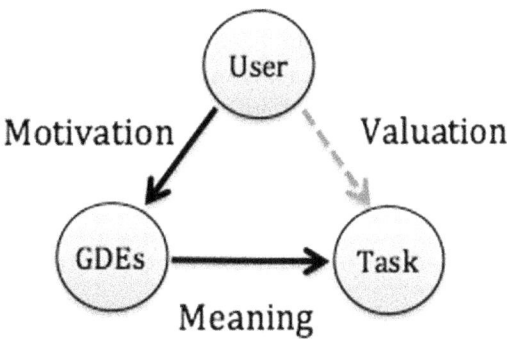

Figure 2. Relationship-based model of effective gamification

> Any gamified system consists of three essential elements: a user, a non-game task for the user to perform, and a set of GDEs that motivate the user to perform the task.

User-GDE Relationship

The User-GDE relationship is one of motivation. In terms of the purpose descriptors from Table 3, this relationship includes motivating users, engaging users, and increasing user interest. The conceptual framework for this relationship is the theory of motivational affordances (Zhang, 2008 and Deterding, 2011), supported by self-determination theory (SDT) (Ryan & Deci, 2002). According to these theories, motivation is afforded when the GDEs align with user abilities, allowing the user to fulfill the basic psychological needs of autonomy, competence, and relatedness (Deterding, 2011). Inherent in this relationship is the concept that users differ. Accordingly, a set of GDEs that provide strong motivational affordances to one user may prove ineffective for another. Two promising methods for supporting the user-GDE relationship are user-centered design (Nicholson, 2012) and adaptive gamification (Monterrat, et al., 2014). Besides accommodating different user types, these methods also increase the challenge associated with the GDEs as a player's mastery increases (Lee & Hammer, 2011).

GDE-Task Relationship

Fundamental to the GDE-Task relationship is the task itself. Like users, tasks are not created equal. The best tasks for gamification are those that have intrinsic value to the user (Deci, et al., 2001). For example, a gamified fitness tracker will be more successful if the user desires to become more fit, and will be even more successful if the GDEs are designed to reinforce that value. Of the purposes listed in Table 3, the GDE-Task relationship is crucial in establishing a gamelike experience. Towards this end, Aparicio and his colleagues (2012) propose a four-step process for effective gamification.

1. Clearly identify the main objective (Task)
2. Identify other objectives that would be interesting to users. These objectives form the foundation upon which the game mechanics are built
3. Select game mechanics (GDEs) that simultaneously support the main objective, the game objectives, and the basic psychological needs of the users
4. Assess the effectiveness of the design

motivation is afforded when the GDEs align with user abilities, allowing the user to fulfill the basic psychological needs of autonomy, competence, and relatedness (Deterding, 2011).

An important aspect of an effective design is *integrating* the GDEs with the task, instead of merely adding them on (Linehan, et al., 2011). A scoring system that simply counts occurrences, for example, will not help the user establish or maintain a meaningful connection with the underlying Task (Nicholson, 2012). A meaningful GDE-Task relationship can also be supported by providing GDEs that allow users to set goals, and then work to achieve those goals (Linehan, et al., 2011). Additionally, the schedule of rewards is also important. According to SDT, rewards are often seen as controlling, which has a detrimental affect on the user's underlying valuation of the task (Ryan & Deci, 2002). However, receiving a reward for having achieved something worthwhile can potentially affirm the user's competence, which would have favorable results (Dichev, et al., 2014).

Like users, tasks are not created equal.

User-Task Relationship

The relationship between the user and the task is summarized by the word *valuation*. The more value the user places on the task, the more effective gamification will be. Similarly, the more motivated the user is to perform the task without gamification, the more effective gamification will be. By definition, the user-task relationship is the reason to gamify a system. If the user is intrinsically motivated to accomplish the task, gamification is not required. Therefore, a gamified system provides needed extrinsic motivation for the user to accomplish the designated task. It is important to note that even if the gamified system is intrinsically motivating to the user, this motivation is directed towards the GDEs and not to the task itself. In other words, the intrinsically motivating GDEs serve as *extrinsic* motivators for the task. According to SDT, a gamified system built entirely on extrinsic motivators will decrease a user's inherent motivation for the task (Ryan & Deci, 2002). If the GDEs are removed, the user will likely be worse off—in terms of being able to accomplish the task—than before the gamification was added (Nicholson, 2012). The underlying theory for this relationship is the SDT sub-theory organismic integration theory (OIT). The goal for long-term effective gamification is not just for the user to accomplish the task, but also for the user to internalize or integrate the task. This is more likely to be accomplished when the gamification system allows for the basic psychological needs of autonomy, competence, and relatedness to be met.

Treasure Hunters: A Case Study

Gamification is not a game, yet when it is applied to an online course or a business's rewards program, it employs game-like properties to increase participation and engagement. To illustrate how gamification can transform an existing course or system into a game, the authors analyzed a case study conducted by Calongne (2005a; 2005b) that featured the design, implementation and assessment of a Treasure Hunter Game to strengthen online learning.

One goal of the study was to reduce the fear that students experience when working in online teams and to strengthen the final project, which was developed by small groups of 3-4 members during two 5.5 week class. The software project management class met fully online while the software requirements engineering class used a hybrid or blended learning model and met one night a week on campus and the rest of the weekly activities were held online. In the hybrid model, students attended a face-to-face class once a week for three hours, and completed their assignments and class discussions online using Blackboard, a learning management tool.

a gamified system provides needed extrinsic motivation for the user to accomplish the designated task.

The problem noted with these classes stemmed from student reluctance to begin work on the team project. Both classes developed team projects: 1) the hybrid class developed a software project management plan with a detailed schedule, an organization breakdown structure, a work breakdown structure, a strategy for defining cost accounts and related elements to support a complex software development project; and 2) the online class developed a software requirements specification with a lifecycle requirements traceability matrix. Working together in groups was a vital part of the career-oriented curriculum as it provided life skills suitable for future work in software engineering. Mapping the course assignments to the game mechanics required preserving the curriculum goals while measuring that the students were developing the desired skills and competencies.

Working together in groups was a vital part of the career-oriented curriculum

In past online and hybrid classes, new students who were unfamiliar with the team project format dreaded working in online classes on the team projects. The instructor noted that they were slow to get oriented and begin the team activities, and spent much of the first few weeks reflecting on the requirements and their individual needs. The learners provided excellent posts during the first week's introductions, but for some students, the difficulty in coordinating team activities reduced the quantity of discussion posts and the energy level seemed to plateau. Past class offerings used different strategies, including assigning students to teams and allowing students to form their own teams. The problem with either team formation strategy was that the team progress was slow and project delays had the risk of increasing stress later in the term and turning the project's activities into a heroic effort on the part of the project's integrator. Using gamification design in the online course rubrics offered opportunities to reduce anxiety, encourage early teamwork and remap the perceptions and beliefs on the value of online teamwork.

It is these values and beliefs combined with the focus on completing the project tasks that illustrate the power of Wilson's models as noted in Figures 1 and 2. Without understanding the perception of learners as players, and finding mechanisms to support their fears and support skill development through routine feedback; the game might have been a light-hearted activity rather than a new way to think about the utility of teamwork in online games.

Gamification Design: Metaphors and Game Mechanics

The game design process featured identifying game metaphors that fit the values and needs of the students (what students wanted) with the necessary tasks (curriculum and course assignments). The game mechanics offered rewards of value to the students (in this case, gold coins) that had a one-to-one relationship with the rubrics and point values used to evaluate progress and assign grades in the course. For example, a 25-point assignment was worth 25 gold coins. Partial completion of the task could earn fewer coins, similar to incomplete work on a class activity. In addition to these direct measurements, the game featured incentives that were advertised and available to each player to encourage the learners to extend themselves as they tried different ways to communicate, collaborate, complete the project tasks and integrate their individual efforts into a cohesive document.

gamification design in the online course rubrics offered opportunities to reduce anxiety, encourage early teamwork and remap the perceptions and beliefs on the value of online teamwork.

While games may encourage awareness and energy through the perception of competition, in online classes that do not grade on a curve, striving for excellence is not limited to the top percent of the class. Yet seeing progress over time and the relationship of user needs with tasks as they were completed creates an energy that adds to the level of excitement in a game. Deci and Ryan (2000) noted that reinforcing a pressure to win may reduce the intrinsic motivation. To reinforce the design to foster lifelong team skills, the players needed a sense of control and autonomy in the game's progress and ownership of the game.

The Treasure Hunter's Report offered progress checks, yet masked the identity and relationship of players through the use of non-player characters (NPCs) added to the class ranks. Protecting the participants' right to privacy and encouraging collegial bonhomie across the different teams were also factors in the gamification design. As a result, incentives for supporting and mentoring other classmates shifted the energy from an overemphasis on the product and the completion of each task to understanding the process of project development and synthesizing it.

Since the classes featured a mix of senior and new students, it was a challenge to assess what each student wanted for rewards prior to class, so a common value system was selected and approved by the class during the first week. When asked during the first class for a preference, they unanimously agreed to use gold and the Treasure Hunter's Game was launched. Other metaphors included a Dragon's Hoard, which described the piles of gold coins as they accumulated, and reputation titles as these metaphorical piles grew taller. When students offered insights that were noteworthy, the instructor typed or said *Ka-ching!* in the feedback, and described the sound of coins flowing into their coffers as she addressed mastery of the concepts.

While it was easy to map gold rewards to discussion posts and normal course activities, to encourage the process as well as good project development practices led to the need for more granular measurements such as: proposing ideas, mentoring discussions, keeping the team updated on the project's status, taking charge of specific sections of the project, and integrating the team's efforts into a

Treasure Hunter Report

Character Name	Score
Daffy Duck	470
Griselda Grinch	465
Freakish Frank	425
Jagged Jane	390
Sam Shorty	345
Scooby Doo	310
Mack McClown	275

cohesive document. This expanded list of measurements added to the instructor's workload, yet took some of the subjectivity out of assessing each player's performance prior to delivery of the final project. Rewards for completing early work, mentoring others and demonstrating leadership exceeded the normal classes' point values, requiring them to be tracked separately in an instrument called The Treasure Hunter's Report. So the game's scoring system mapped to the course's gradebook, but offered more extensive measurements and exceeded the course's total points. To ensure

---

players needed a sense of control and autonomy in the game's progress and ownership of the game.

FERPA compliance, each player provided a game alias that was unknown to the other students. The instructor added a variety of game non-player characters (NPCs) to the list with at least two at the top, two in the mid-range and two at the bottom. Using a *"run with the pack"* competition strategy modeled after the animal kingdom, the goal was to have an unknown set of NPCs encouraging the top, bottom and mid-range players to continue to strive for excellence. The Treasure Hunter Report featured each student who participated in the game (all but one in the hybrid class and all of them in the online class) and the NPCs, but without the students realizing that some of the names were not classmates. This was important to preserve anonymity and to encourage players at all levels to strive for excellence.

Analysis of the Treasure Hunter Case Study

The evaluation of the collected data focused on studying whether the course and learning objectives were met and if they satisfied the program outcomes. The goal was to strengthen two fast track graduate classes and foster better team experiences. As the game centered on the use of normal class activities using game-based metaphors, the course assessment method was a natural choice for evaluating whether the game constructs met the desired course outcomes. The Treasure Hunter's Game had five goals in addition to the course objectives:
1. participation early and often in the course
2. encouraging contributions with substantive content
3. promoting collaboration and team communication skills
4. providing traceability for individual activity on the team project
5. encouraging successful team outcomes with measurable competencies

Since the number of graded measurements grew from weekly assignments to over 25 measurements, the students were free to work ahead or to spend more time on desired activities, and in response, their treasure grew and their game status rose as they progressed through the team activities. A set of game titles mapped to the different reputation levels, giving the gamers roles and a way of characterizing and visualizing their accomplishments. The energy shifted from the perception of routine course work to their demands for more opportunities to earn gold and faster publication of the treasure report.

> **The goal was to strengthen two fast track graduate classes and foster better team experiences.**

Case Study Results

The results are separated by each goal and type of class delivery method, which featured a hybrid class that met one day a week in the classroom with the discussions and activity online, and a fully online class. The difference between them featured the ability for the hybrid class offering of the software requirements engineering class to hold a face-to-face team meeting after class while the online class never met in class. They both had the class area in the online course management system for posting team discussions, assignments and their learning artifacts. See Table 4 for a comparison of the results for the hybrid and online class when compared to prior class offerings.

Goal 1: Increased participation:

The hybrid class featured the development of a software project management plan and 88% of the 25-member class was enthusiastic contributors,

Table 4
Case study results as compared to prior class offerings on the quality and volume of discussion posts, % completing three project status reports and % completing peer reviews of team members

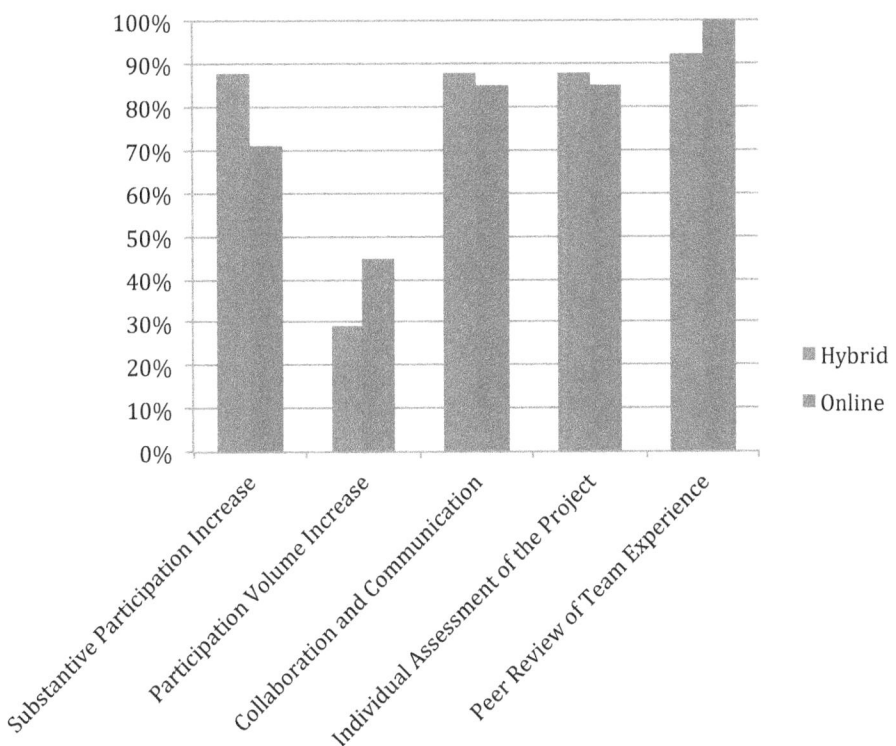

participating early and often. The remaining 12% rose in the game ranks midway through the course due to delays from medical and other life stresses, and they quickly caught up with the other participants.

The fully online class featured two teams that developed a software requirements specification with a requirements traceability matrix. Of the seven class members, 71% of them posted earlier and with substantive content as compared to past online class offerings. In addition to using the course management system's discussion board and team area, some of the students traveled to meet face-to-face and shared the results of those meetings while others held online voice conferences and invited the instructor. This was not required, but an observation on their preference.

Goal 2: Higher rates of participation

In both the hybrid and online classes, the volume of posts increased 29%-45% as noted in a comparison from prior sections of the same classes and throughout the five weeks of discussion forums for both the hybrid or online course design, and both classes posted their final projects a week earlier than past classes with one notable exception. One exception was noted. In a term prior to the Treasure Hunter's Game, a group of software professionals who worked together on the same team worked on a team project and posted their project a week early.

Goal 3: Collaboration and communication

Students completed project status reports in prior classes, but due to the time constraints and a poor understanding of how to complete them, most posted only one status report. During the case study, every student in the hybrid and online case study classes completed two of the project status reports, and in the hybrid class, 88% completed a third report, and in the online class, 85% completed a third report. A critic might observe that without the game's rewards, their desire to keep their teammates informed on the project's progress might have been less detailed.

Goal 4: Individual Assessment of Team Project Activities

While it is common to assign a team grade for a shared project, past classes featured assigned duties on the project and discrete measurements for tracking participation, project decisions, task completion and progress. These individual measurements mirrored the process of project development in the workplace and the status reports featured each team member's status with regard to the Progress, Plans and Problems related to specific project sections.

Ensuring a cohesive project that demonstrates the use of a replicable process is not easy with novice learners, and they need opportunities to fail and discover alternative strategies. In games, failure is often a barrier to success that is overcome through trying new strategies and learning from past mistakes. These same strategies were used in the project development. In the hybrid class, the instructor played the role of a person who was ill-informed on the project's goals and process. As the presumed fount of all knowledge, the instructor would offer outrageous advice and give insights into common myths that invade everyday practices.

The students as players were encouraged to point out the problems with these "helpful" tips and to take a leadership role to guide, inform, modify and in some cases, strengthen the process used during project development. In the online class, 85% completed all of the bonus activities, sharing the leadership role and keeping their teams informed on the project's progress. 88% of the hybrid class completed most of the bonus activities, but not all of them. This may be due to their weekly face-to-face meetings and other mechanisms for sharing information.

Goal 5: Successful Team Experience and Team Project

A peer evaluation was completed prior to submitting the project, and on it, each team member rated the contributions of their teammates and noted how they had contributed. These peer reviews were also worth gold coins and provided another perspective for assessing the value of each team member's contributions. Increased satisfaction and perceptions of the process and value of online teamwork featured highly during the feedback from the class, and over 30% of the participants asked for more quests once the class ended. They did not want to stop playing at the end of the course. While indirect, it was one of the more powerful insights from the experience.

Treasure Hunt Case Study Conclusions

Linking the process (the game with a team of players) with the product (online learning and the development of the team project) was a great success. In spite of the fanciful metaphors, it was popular, and the students demanded faster progress reports and were eager to see the results of their efforts. Tabulating on the Treasure Hunter Report was a manual process that featured a few strategies to maintain privacy and to motivate the players. As previously mentioned, at each level at least two NPCs ranked with the top, bottom and mid-range players, reinforcing "running with the pack." To reduce the likelihood of NPC detection, their growth could only advance in a reasonable fashion given the possible measurements and incentives for that week. In some cases, the list was scrambled with the rank order switched from low-to-high or high-to-low while at other times, it featured other elements. Only aliases were displayed and only if they remained anonymous. The team members were "sworn to secrecy" and encouraged to keep their reputation titles to themselves. No one mentioned them in class, except to say that they enjoyed advancing through the ranks and having their accomplishments reinforced. From an instructor's perspective, implementing the game required planning and steady work. During the last three weeks, the students as players insisted on daily if not hourly reports, and future games of this nature will benefit from an automated gamification process and report generation.

Grades are insufficient catalysts for ensuring great online team experiences. Without recognizing the beliefs and values that learners bring to class as they work on the online team projects, it would be hard to help them remap these perceptions with new perspectives. The game-design elements were simple in the case study and the overhead was mostly in keeping track of the measurements on a spreadsheet and the metaphors for creating energy and excitement in the game.

As Wilson (2015) observed, how the game is designed is only one piece of the puzzle. Motivating the learners, getting everyone energized and hosting a great game requires a great implementation and hard work, at least initially. Once the learners assume ownership of the game, the burden on the instructor shifts and the game feels like an organic part of the class and quite natural.

Linking the process (the game with a team of players) with the product (online learning and the development of the team project) was a great success.

Back to the Future Research

The case study offered individual measurements in the game for team activities, but several opportunities emerged during the assessment phase. For the educational use of gamification, future work could explore the opportunities presented by collaborative gamification to strengthen the team experience through shared goals, measurements, collaboration tasks, group communication mechanisms and in fostering team cohesion for online learning.

Gamification as self-determined learning is a goal within heutagogy, and it presents opportunities for encouraging the development of lifelong learning skills and students as game designers. In past classes, andragogy was a common learning strategy as students would use trial and error to map their prior knowledge to new experiences and review the content only when their behaviors was not supported.

Several opportunities for future work are indicated. Through gamification, it may be possible to blend how adults learn (andragogy) with self-determined learning (heutagogy) to offer insights on how to enhance knowledge and skill development through online learning. Ethnographic studies that follow the gamers through time and over several courses may discover insights useful for future work. How to transfer the energy and ownership of the game to the students as players through game ownership may lead to interesting research in shared leadership and peer mentorship.
As learning involves certain challenges, future work may explore the strategies for achieving game balance to meet curriculum requirements and how to maintain game balance by keeping the challenge level slightly higher than the skill level of its players. The Flow Model (Csikszentmihalyi, 1975; Hoffman & Novak, 2009) is one instrument for examining the gamer's perceptions and emotions as they face new challenges and attempt to develop their skills through gamification.

Through gamification, it may be possible to blend how adults learn (andragogy) with self-determined learning (heutagogy) to offer insights on how to enhance knowledge and skill development through online learning.

Conclusion

Gamification offers the promise of better online learning experiences with regard to early work and effective teamwork. Through the use of game-based mechanics, it can encourage learners to participate, collaborate and develop effective online team skills. But there are no guarantees that the use of game design in an online course will lead to success.

Future successes in this area will come from careful planning and design; from selecting game mechanics and rewards that map to the beliefs and values of the participants, and for selecting metaphors and game characteristics that support how the players feel about the tasks and their importance. By blending user interaction design strategies with game-based mechanics and a sensitivity for what motivates the participants, achieving the desired outcomes through a great gamification experience is within reach.

Gamification offers the promise of better online learning experiences

References

Anderson, A., Huttenlocher, D., Kleinberg, J., & Leskovec, J. (2013). Steering user behavior with badges. Paper presented at the Proceedings of the 22nd international conference on World Wide Web.

Aparicio, A. F., Vela, F. L. G., Sánchez, J. L. G., & Montes, J. L. I. (2012). Analysis and application of gamification. Paper presented at the Proceedings of the 13th International Conference on Interacción Persona-Ordenador.

Bagley, K. S. (2012). Conceptual mile markers to improve time-to-value for exploratory search sessions. Doctoral dissertation, University of Massachusetts Lowell. ISBN: 978-1-267-95293-6.

Bista, S. K., Nepal, S., Colineau, N., & Paris, C. (2012). Using gamification in an online community. Paper presented at the Collaborative Computing: Networking, Applications and Worksharing (CollaborateCom), 2012 8th International Conference.

Bista, S. K., Nepal, S., & Paris, C. (2012). Engagement and Cooperation in Social Networks: Do Benefits and Rewards Help? Paper presented at the 2012 IEEE 11th International Conference on Trust, Security and Privacy in Computing and Communications (TrustCom).

Cafazzo, J. A., Casselman, M., Hamming, N., Katzman, D. K., & Palmert, M. R. (2012). Design of an mHealth app for the self-management of adolescent type 1 diabetes: a pilot study. *Journal of Medical Internet Research, 14*(3), e70.

Calongne, C. (2005a). Let's Play: Using Game Design in Our Online Course Rubrics, TCC 2005 Worldwide Online Conference, April 19-21, 2005. Retrieved February 24, 2007 from http://tcc.kcc.hawaii.edu/previous/TCC%202005/calongne02.pdf

Calongne, C. (2005b). Playing to Enhance Learning: Using Game Design in Our Online Course Rubrics, TCC 2005 Worldwide Online Conference, April 19-21, 2005. Retrieved from http://tcc.kcc.hawaii.edu/previous/TCC%202005/calongne.pdf

Cheong, C., Cheong, F., Filippou, J., Lee, J.-N., Mao, J.-Y., & Thong, J. (2013). Quick quiz: A gamified approach for enhancing learning. PACIS 2013, 1.

Csikszentmihalyi, M. (2008). *Flow: The psychology of optimal experience.* New York, NY: Harper Collins e-books.

Deci, E.L. & Ryan, R.M. (2000). Self-determination theory and the facilitation of intrinsic motivation, social development, and well-being. *American Psychologist, Vol 55*(1), pp 68-78. http://dx.doi.org/10.1037/0003-066X.55.1.68

Deci, E. L., Koestner, R., & Ryan, R. M. (2001). Extrinsic rewards and intrinsic motivation in education: Reconsidered once again. *Review of Educational Research, 71*(1), 1-27.

Denny, P. (2013). The effect of virtual achievements on student engagement. Paper presented at the Proceedings of the SIGCHI Conference on Human Factors in Computing Systems.

Depura, K., & Garg, M. (2012). Application of online gamification to new hire onboarding. Paper presented at the 2012 Third International Conference on Services in Emerging Markets (ICSEM).

Deterding, S. (2011). Situated motivational affordances of game elements: A conceptual model. Paper presented at the Gamification: Using Game Design Elements in Non-Gaming Contexts, a workshop at CHI.

Deterding, S., Dixon, D., Khaled, R., & Nacke, L. (2011). From game design elements to gamefulness: defining gamification.

Paper presented at the Proceedings of the 15th International Academic MindTrek Conference: Envisioning Future Media Environments.

Dichev, C., Dicheva, D., Angelova, G., & Agre, G. (2014). From Gamification to Gameful Design and Gameful Experience in Learning. *Cybernetics And Information Technologies, 14*(4).

Domínguez, A., Saenz-de-Navarrete, J., De-Marcos, L., Fernández-Sanz, L., Pagés, C., & Martínez-Herráiz, J.-J. (2013). Gamifying learning experiences: Practical implications and outcomes. *Computers & Education, 63*, 380-392.

Downes-Le Guin, T., Baker, R., Mechling, J., & Ruylea, E. (2012). Myths and realities of respondent engagement in online surveys. *International Journal of Market Research, 54*(5), 1-21.

Fitz-Walter, Z., Tjondronegoro, D., & Wyeth, P. (2011). Orientation passport: using gamification to engage university students. Paper presented at the Proceedings of the 23rd Australian Computer-Human Interaction Conference.

Fitz-Walter, Z., Tjondronegoro, D., & Wyeth, P. (2012). A gamified mobile application for engaging new students at university orientation. Paper presented at the Proceedings of the 24th Australian Computer-Human Interaction Conference.

Flatla, D. R., Gutwin, C., Nacke, L. E., Bateman, S., & Mandryk, R. L. (2011). Calibration games: making calibration tasks enjoyable by adding motivating game elements. Paper presented at the Proceedings of the 24th annual ACM symposium on User interface software and technology.

Foster, J. A., Sheridan, P. K., Irish, R., & Frost, G. S. (2012). Gamification as a strategy for promoting deeper investigation in a reverse engineering activity. Paper presented at the American Society for Engineering Education.

Frith, J. H. (2012). Constructing location, one check-in at a time: Examining the practices of foursquare users: North Carolina State University.

Gnauk, B., Dannecker, L., & Hahmann, M. (2012). Leveraging gamification in demand dispatch systems. Paper presented at the Proceedings of the 2012 Joint EDBT/ICDT Workshops.

Goehle, G. (2013). Gamification and web-based homework. *Primus, 23*(3), 234-246.

Grant, S., & Betts, B. (2013). Encouraging user behaviour with achievements: an empirical study. Paper presented at the 2012 Third International Conference on Mining Software Repositories (MSR).

Hakulinen, L., Auvinen, T., & Korhonen, A. (2013). Empirical study on the effect of achievement badges in TRAKLA2 online learning environment. Paper presented at the Learning and Teaching in Computing and Engineering (LaTiCE), 2013.

Hamari, J. (2013). Transforming homo economicus into homo ludens: A field experiment on gamification in a utilitarian peer-to-peer trading service. Electronic commerce research and applications, 12(4), 236-245.

Hamari, J., & Koivisto, J. (2013). Social motivations to use gamification: an empirical study of gamifying exercise. Proceedings of the European Conference on Information

Systems, June 5-8, 2013, Utrecht, The Netherlands.

Hamari, J., Koivisto, J., & Sarsa, H. (2014). Does Gamification Work?--A Literature Review of Empirical Studies on Gamification. Paper presented at the 2014 47th Hawaii International Conference on System Sciences (HICSS).

Hori, Y., Tokuda, Y., Miura, T., Hiyama, A., & Hirose, M. (2013). Communication pedometer: a discussion of gamified communication focused on frequency of smiles. Paper presented at the Proceedings of the 4th Augmented Human International Conference.

Hoffman, D. & Novak, T. (2009). Flow online: Lessons learned and future prospects. *Journal of Interactive Marketing, 23*(2009), 23-34.

Huizinga, J. (1955) *Homo ludens: a study in the play element in culture*. Boston, MA: Beacon Press.

Huotari, K., & Hamari, J. (2012). Defining gamification: a service marketing perspective. Paper presented at the Proceeding of the 16th International Academic MindTrek Conference.

Igel, C., & Urquhart, V. (2012). Generation Z, meet cooperative learning. *Middle School Journal, 43*(4), 16-21. Retrieved from http://search.proquest.com/docview/1282264478?accountid=8289

Lee, J. J., & Hammer, J. (2011). Gamification in education: What, how, why bother? *Academic Exchange Quarterly, 15*(2), 146.

Li, W., Grossman, T., & Fitzmaurice, G. (2012). Gamicad: a gamified tutorial system for first time autocad users. Paper presented at the Proceedings of the 25th annual ACM symposium on User interface software and technology.

Linehan, C., Kirman, B., Lawson, S., & Chan, G. (2011). Practical, appropriate, empirically-validated guidelines for designing educational games. Paper presented at the Proceedings of the SIGCHI Conference on Human Factors in Computing Systems.

Liu, Y., Alexandrova, T., & Nakajima, T. (2011). Gamifying intelligent environments. Paper presented at the Proceedings of the 2011 international ACM workshop on Ubiquitous meta user interfaces.

Massung, E., Coyle, D., Cater, K. F., Jay, M., & Preist, C. (2013). Using crowdsourcing to support pro-environmental community activism. Paper presented at the Proceedings of the SIGCHI Conference on Human Factors in Computing Systems.

Monterrat, B., Lavoué, É., & George, S. (2014). *A Framework to Adapt Gamification in Learning Environments Open Learning and Teaching in Educational Communities* (pp. 578-579): Springer

Nicholson, S. (2012). A user-centered theoretical framework for meaningful gamification. *Games+Learning+Society, 8*, 1.

Passos, E. B., Medeiros, D. B., Neto, P. A., & Clua, E. W. (2011). Turning real-world software development into a game. Paper presented at the 2011 Brazilian Symposium on Games and Digital Entertainment (SBGAMES).

Posnick-Goodwin, S. (2010). Meet Generation Z. CTA Magazine, 14(5). Retrieved from http://www.cta.org/Professional-Development/Publications/Educator-Feb-10/Meet-Generation-Z.aspx

Ryan, R., & Deci, E. L. (2002). Overview of self-determination theory: An organismic dialectical perspective. *Handbook of self-determination research*, 3-33.

Salen Tekinbas, K. & Zimmerman, E. (2003). *Rules of play: Game design fundamentals*. Cambridge, MA: MIT Press.

Schell, J. (2014). *The Art of game design: a Book of lenses* (2nd ed.). Boca Raton, FL: CRC Press.

Seaborn, K., & Fels, D. I. (2015). Gamification in theory and action: A survey. *International Journal of Human-Computer Studies, 74*, 14-31.

Smith, A.-L., & Baker, L. (2011). Getting a clue: creating student detectives and dragon slayers in your library. *Reference Services Review, 39*(4), 628-642.

Thom, J., Millen, D., & DiMicco, J. (2012). Removing gamification from an enterprise SNS. Paper presented at the Proceedings of the ACM 2012 conference on Computer Supported Cooperative Work.

Wilson, D. (2015). Engagement vs. valuation: two levels of gamification effectiveness, a design model [Unpublished doctoral dissertation]. Colorado Technical University, Colorado Springs, Colorado.

Witt, M., Scheiner, C., & Robra-Bissantz, S. (2011). Gamification of online idea competitions: Insights from an explorative case. *Informatik schafft Communities*, 192.

Zhang, P. (2008). Technical opinion Motivational affordances: reasons for ICT design and use. *Communications of the ACM, 51*(11), 145-147.

Definitions

1. Gamification: the use of game-design elements (e.g. badges, turns, goals, challenges, playtesting) in non-game contexts (e.g. education, marketing, exercise, innovation)
2. Game design elements: the components and mechanics of games, as well as the principles, models, and methods of game design. Examples include: badges, turns, goals, challenges, and playtesting
3. Gamification design model: three essential elements of a gamified system: a user, a set of game design elements, and a task. The model also includes the relationships between these elements: motivation, meaning, and valuation
4. Game elements: the components and mechanics of games, such as points, badges, turns, and limited resources
5. Generation Z: That segment of the population born between 1990 and early 2000s.

Advanced Faculty Professional Development for Online Course Building: An Action Research Project

Philip Aust,[A] Griselda Thomas,[B] Tamara Powell,[C] Christopher K. Randall,[D] Vanessa Slinger-Friedman,[E] Joe Terantino,[F] and Tiffani Reardon[G]

> *This article reports on an action research project conducted by an Office of Distance Education at Kennesaw State University (KSU) for the purpose of finding a solution to the professional development of* advanced *faculty technology users. Action research (Lewin, 1946) involves a cycle of planning, action, and subsequent research to determine the effects of a social action. In particular, this research uses developmental action inquiry to gain knowledge "through action and for action" (Torbert, 2002; Torbert, 2004). Accordingly, this study identifies a problem, plans and implements a solution, and determines the effectiveness of that solution. Thus, three distance learning directors and 10 departmental online coordinators in KSU's College of Humanities and Social Sciences (HSS) created and alpha tested an online training program for faculty with* advanced *technology experience. The group then beta tested the program and analyzed faculty responses for conceptual themes to revise the program. The revised online training program was then updated and offered to HSS faculty. The effect of this training is discussed in terms of its impact on the number of new online courses developed over the past few years in HSS at KSU.*
>
> **Keywords:** *advanced faculty development, online faculty training, pedagogy, professional development, online learning, elearning, action research*

[A] **Dr. Philip Aust** is an Associate Professor at Kennesaw State University (KSU) in the School of Communication & Media. He serves as Communication's Online Coordinator for KSU's College of Humanities and Social Sciences. With 25 years of university instructional experience, Dr. Aust regularly teaches Communication & Media's Master of Arts Program Capstone Course as well as Leadership Communication, Interpersonal Communication, and Communication Research Methods at the undergraduate level using face-to-face, hybrid, and online formats. His research interests include leadership in professional contexts, educational technology, and online instructional communication.

[B] **Dr. Griselda Thomas** is an Associate Professor of English and Interdisciplinary Studies, and the Coordinator of the African and African Diaspora Studies Program at Kennesaw State University. The former Online Coordinator for Interdisciplinary Studies teaches face-to-face, hybrid, and online courses in African American literature and culture, and African and African Diaspora studies. Her research and publications explore online pedagogy, the fiction of contemporary Black women writers and cultural influences in the Black community. Dr. Thomas received her PhD in African American Studies from Temple University in 2008, where she also earned a MA in African American Studies and a Graduate Certificate in Women's Studies. She received a MA in English from Northeastern University.

[C] **Dr. Tamara Powell** is the Director of the College of Humanities and Social Sciences Office of Distance Education and an Associate Professor of English at Kennesaw State University. Her research interests include strategies to increase student retention, satisfaction, and success in online courses.

[D] **Christopher K. Randall** is an Associate Professor of Psychology, Assistant Chair, and Departmental Online Coordinator at Kennesaw State University. He previously served as Associate Director for Technology-Enhanced Learning in the Center for Excellence in Teaching and Learning at KSU and has held various academic adminis-

doi: 10.18278/il.4.2.11

Introduction

Allen and Seaman's (2014) report of online education in the United States (U.S.) continues to establish the Internet's increasing role in higher education. Their latest installment expands on three trends advanced in their tenth annual report (Allen & Seaman, 2013). First, Allen and Seaman confirm the number of U.S. institutions offering online courses continues to climb. While the "vast majority of higher education (71.7%) institutions had some form of online offering" in 2002, today that number stands at 86.5 percent (p. 20). In short, it is now rare for a U.S. university not to offer coursework online.

Second, Allen and Seaman note the number of public and private online university degree programs offered in the U.S. continues to grow. The number of degree programs offered fully online jumped from "48.9% of U.S. institutions in 2002 to 70.6% in 2012" (Allen & Seaman, 2013, p. 21). In the last decade alone online private nonprofit degree programs in the U.S. have more than doubled from "22.1% in 2002 to 48.4% in 2012" (p. 21). Even small, residential, liberal arts colleges are looking to online learning to give their students summer and study abroad flexibility. In short, no sector is immune to the growth of online learning.

Third, Allen and Seaman report the number of students taking online courses in the U.S. continues to increase. Whereas less than 10 percent of students in the U.S. were taking an online course in 2002, that percentage stood "at 32 percent" in 2012 (Allen & Seaman, 2013, p. 4). This increase is particularly noteworthy because while the number of students enrolled in higher education *fell* in 2012, the number of those taking online courses *rose* to 6.7 million. These findings illustrate how fast higher education has changed as institutions have worked to make the web a classroom.

One way researchers have analyzed online education is by way of the different parties impacted by it (e.g., students, faculty, and universities). Although students have received the bulk of attention to date in the literature—and justifiably so—attention has also been given to the instructor. In

---

trative posts at other institutions. Chris has been teaching technology-enhanced and fully online courses since 1998. Consequently, his current research interests focus on the pedagogy of online teaching and learning.

[E] **Dr. Vanessa Slinger-Friedman** is an Associate Professor of Geography and Associate Director of Distance Education for the College of Humanities and Social Sciences at Kennesaw State University. Originally from Trinidad, Dr. Slinger-Friedman obtained her M.A. in Latin American Studies and Ph.D. in Geography from the University of Florida. An area of research interest for Dr. Slinger-Friedman is innovative pedagogy and online teaching.

[F] **Dr. Joe Terantino** is Associate Professor of Foreign Language Education & Spanish, co-Director of the Master of Arts in Foreign Languages, and Director of the Foreign Language Resource Center. His expertise lies in teaching methodology, second language acquisition, distance learning, and computer-assisted language learning. He is a passionate user and researcher of instructional technology, distance learning, and social media who enjoys the challenge of tinkering with new technologies. In particular, he is interested in computer-assisted language learning, foreign language education, and the integration of technology in teaching.

[G] **Tiffani Reardon** is an instructional designer at Kennesaw State University. She has a Bachelor of Arts in English from KSU and is currently working toward a Master of Science in Instructional Design and Technology from Georgia State University. Her research interests include instructional design and technology, technical writing, online learning, web design, and foreign languages. Tiffani also works freelance as a web designer under the name eTiff Designs out of her home where she lives with her Yorkie-Poo, Nutmeg, and her partner, Josh in Acworth, Ga.

reality, university instructors have been in the crosshairs for over a decade now as they have had to update their skills in order to take on the duties associated with educating students online. This shift in pedagogy is significant. University-level instructors have had to adjust to the online environment, while learning a range of new technologies in order to ensure their online courses achieve the same learning outcomes as face-to-face education. Not surprisingly, Paulus, Myers, Mixer, Wyatt, Lee, and Lee (2010) assert that more research must be done to equip faculty with the means to teach effectively online. Paulus et al. assert that faculty development programs are where this training occurs. Likewise, Roth (2014) advances that higher education must understand instructional professional development because of the vital role faculty members play in ensuring quality education for students completing online courses.

With so much at stake, it is surprising that there is not more research on faculty training programs designed to equip instructors to teach online, although more has emerged in recent years. Still there is notably little research on faculty development programs for instructors with existing experience teaching online but who desire advanced instructional skills. Subsequently, this study focuses on the professional development of university-level faculty with some experience in online teaching, but who seek greater expertise. The next section establishes what literature offers in this area.

Literature Review

A literature review was conducted to determine what research currently indicates about faculty training for online instruction. Three trends emerged from this literature: First, training programs are consistently developed, conducted, and analyzed based on a distinct theoretical framework. Second, a range of case studies on faculty training for online course development has been conducted. And third, this line of inquiry has given considerable attention to best practices of faculty training for online instruction. A synopsis of the first trend follows.

The Online Instruction Training Program Framework

A portion of faculty training research has identified and tested different developmental frameworks for online instruction. Online instruction programs have employed blended online learning, design-based research, and problem-based training as frameworks for faculty development. Nerlich, Soldner, and Millington (2012), Shattuck and Anderson (2013), and Cho and Rathbun (2013) offer examples of these guiding frames.

Nerlich, Soldner, and Millington (2012) employ *Blended Online Learning* (BOL) as their theoretical frame. They choose BOL for several reasons (e.g., to encourage collaboration among faculty members participating in online instructional training), but most importantly because BOL promotes a "community of inquiry" among trainees (p. 323). Based on Nerlich et al.'s research, BOL is found useful for building and facilitating faculty training because it positively impacts those at most, if not all, levels of higher education (e.g., the student, the teacher, and the administrator). Further, BOL is deemed valuable because it helps facilitate trainee collaboration and problem-solving abilities during training as well as after a program has ended.

In contrast, Shattuck and Anderson (2013) identify *design-based research* (DBR) as their framework for training in order to maximize the skill development of part-time instructors enrolled in Maryland's Certificate for Online Adjunct Teaching (COAT) course. DBR is "a systematic but flexible methodology aimed to improve educational practices through iterative analysis, design, development and implementation based on collaboration among researchers and practitioners in real-world settings" (Wang & Hannafin, 2005, pp. 6-7). According to Cohen, Manion, and Morrison (2007), DBR is particularly useful for understanding, improving, and reforming established teaching practices. In Shattuck and Anderson's (2013) inquiry, they used DBR as a lens to examine instructors who were preparing to teach online for the first time. Shattuck and Anderson's findings indicate that faculty members responded well to training using DBR based on participant responses. Shattuck and Anderson report that participants found the transition to online instruction much like throwing a pebble in a pond—every decision had a ripple effect on every other part of online teaching. Moreover, trainees made clear that preparing for online training required that they think about all aspects of course development, aspects often overlooked in the classroom. Trainees also stated that online instruction made them think differently about how they approached classroom instruction. In short, faculty training using DBR was deemed relevant and valuable.

Additionally, Cho and Rathbun (2013) chose *problem-based learning* (PBL) as their framework for faculty online training to develop and facilitate a teacher professional development program. Cho and Rathbun specifically selected PBL so trainees would take the initiative to work through the problems associated with teaching online, and they would share what they learn after solving a problem. In their analysis, Cho and Rathbun gave particular attention to trainee responses to assigned tasks, what trainees thought of the resources provided in the program, and how examples of online instruction shared during the program impacted faculty member learning. Based on their research, Cho and Rathbun contend that online teacher development training programs must make two things clear: the expectations of a program before training begins and the role of the trainer during training. They point out that any online training program must be offered at the right time so faculty members not only choose to participate but also take full advantage of it.

Along with Nerlich, Soldner, and Millington (2012), Shattuck and Anderson (2013), and Cho and Rathbun (2013), Baran and Correia's (2014) *nested approach* (i.e., faculty development is a product of several layers of university support) and Fink's (2007) *recognition and reward* model (i.e., faculty must have incentive to teach online; see Hermann, 2013) are also frameworks for developing, managing, and analyzing a faculty training program. In addition to the research distinguishing various frameworks for faculty online training, a portion of the literature consists of case studies on faculty training for online teaching.

Case Studies on Professional Development for Online Teaching

A second theme of faculty development and online teaching literature involves case studies. Barker (2003), Paulus, Myers, Mixer, Wyatt, Lee, and Lee (2011), and Healy, Block, and Judge (2014) have each considered the construction and facilitation of faculty training for online teaching as dealt with at different institutions. Their findings are revealing.

In her article, Barker (2003) describes the steps taken by Sacred Heart University's Nursing Department to offer asynchronous computer-based instruction to departmental faculty. In this case study, Barker generally asserts that faculty training programs must prioritize education first and technology skill development second to be effective. In particular, Barker notes four areas that need attention when considering faculty development for online learning: (a) obtain faculty buy-in up front; (b) emphasize student learning over faculty teaching; (c) stress instructional design and mastery of technology; and (d) highlight the importance of increased opportunity for faculty-student interaction (e.g., through discussion boards). Barker points out that while online learning may seem like a 24/7 proposition, when faculty members set parameters and follow-up with students in a timely manner, online education rivals classroom learning in promoting critical thinking.

Separately, Healy, Block, and Judge's (2014) case study of certified adapted physical educators (CAPEs) aimed to identify the advantages and disadvantages of offering an online faculty training program to university-level educators. The quantitative and qualitative analysis of 42 respondents established that participants viewed online training as an effective means of teacher skill development because it provided greater flexibility (e.g., convenient meeting times, less travel) and increased learning opportunities (e.g., better access to experts and resources); however, participants also noted that online training programs limited the social interaction of trainer with trainees and trainees with trainees. Further, faculty reported that training can suffer when technological problems arise. Healy, Block, and Judge's findings support previous research by Navarro and Shoemaker (1999), Lin and Davidson (1995), Sujo de Montes and Gonzales (2000), and Dede, Ketelhut, Whitehouse, Breit, and McCloskey (2009) all showing that online training has advantages and disadvantages.

More recently, Paulus, Myers, Mixer, Wyatt, Lee, and Lee (2011) reported the results of their case study on nurses transitioning to online instruction at a university in the south. The researchers analyzed the results of a semester long program based on two guiding questions: "What happened during this professional development program…as faculty transitioned to online instructor?" (Paulus et al., p. 2) and "What were… participant experiences in the program?" (p. 2). Their findings include: (a) faulty had difficulty keeping up with training because of the amount of time training required, (b) faculty noted the transition to online teaching produced anxiety, mainly because online teaching varies the learning process, and (c) faculty were concerned with maintaining the momentum of what they learned once the program ended.

In short, this literature makes clear the unique challenges of teaching online as evident in each case study. It highlights how faculty and programs have addressed the challenges of transitioning to online teaching. With this established, a final theme of faculty training and online instruction literature is addressed.

Best Practices for Faculty Training of Online Teachers

Along with literature emphasizing a theoretical framework for building and conducting research and case studies on faculty training programs, this literature has also given attention to best practices of faculty training for online instruction. Gregory and Salmon (2013) and Roth (2014) illustrate this trend in the literature.

Gregory and Salmon (2013) contend that too often faculty training programs are limited because they focus on knowledge and skills of online teaching rather than beliefs and practices. To address this shortcoming, Gregory and Salmon take an intervention approach whereby a mentor-mentee relationship is established during training and continued after the training. Their results produce four principles of training for online instruction. They include: (a) adapt training as needed, (b) make sure training takes context into consideration, (c) spread the word about training, and (d) take steps to ensure on-the-job training.

Likewise, Roth (2014) contends that learning communities are integral to instructor development at the university level. Among his points on effective faculty training for online teaching, Roth advances that: (a) collaboration is integral to effective teaching development, (b) learning communities work best when their purpose are clearly articulated, (c) professional development of teachers is now needed more than ever because of increased technology in higher education, and (d) theory and practice are cornerstones of effective development programs.

In sum, although some research has been done on faculty training for online instruction, more is needed. With the discourse initiated here and offered by others contributing to this line of inquiry (e.g., Wildavsky, Kelly, & Carey, 2011), this research extends faculty development inquiry for online instruction. In particular, this study examines a newly-developed faculty training program designed for instructors with advanced online teaching experience (i.e., faculty who already teach online but who are willing to adopt new technologies and adapt new frameworks to better serve students).

Method

This research employs action research as its method to assess the development of a professional training program for faculty members with existing online teaching experience, but who desire further technology training. Lewin (1946) describes action research as "a comparative research on the conditions and effects of various forms of social action and research leading to social action" (p. 202-203). Within this approach to research is a cycle of planning, actions, and subsequent research to determine the effects of the "social action." Accordingly, this research (a) identifies a problem, (b) plans and implements a solution, and (c) determines the effectiveness of the solution. In particular, the action research described here adheres to developmental action inquiry (Torbert, 2004) in which knowledge is gained "through action and for action" (Torbert, 2002, www.williamrtorbert.com/).

At Kennesaw State University (KSU), the College of Humanities and Social Sciences (CHSS) offers more online courses than any other college in the university. The CHSS Office of Distance Education (ODE) is made up of an instructional designer, nine departmental online coordinators (one from each department), a mobile online coordinator, two assistant directors, and a director. CHSS ODE supports the faculty by, among other things, running the "Build a Web Course Workshop." The workshop is a semester-long faculty development workshop delivered in a hybrid format and covering online pedagogy, course design, the Quality Matters (QM) rubric, online course delivery, and instructional technology. A faculty member successfully completes the workshop when he or she has an online or hybrid course that meets QM standards. Faculty members who successfully complete the workshop and build the online or hybrid course to QM standards receive a $3000 stipend. The workshop began in spring 2010 and by spring 2015, 195 faculty members had successfully completed the "Build a Web Course" workshop.

While the mission of CHSS ODE is to grow online programs and online and hybrid courses, ODE does not promote that growth by compensating faculty solely for course development. Instead, ODE provides a stipend for professional development that includes a *deliverable* (i.e., an online or hybrid course or component of a course). In 2010, when the workshop first began, CHSS administrators theorized that if faculty were taught to build online and hybrid courses with an incentive for the training, then faculty would continue to build and teach more online and hybrid courses.

Statement of the Problem

Although online and hybrid course offerings have increased in CHSS, the rate of increase has not been as significant as that anticipated at the beginning of this study. When faculty members were informally queried regarding the reason, three main answers were given (Terantino, Slinger-Friedman, Thomas, Randall, Aust, & Powell, 2014; Slinger-Friedman, Terantino, Randall, Aust, & Powell, 2014.) First, they wanted updated online/hybrid teaching skills. While faculty could take the workshop or any part of it as many times as they liked, they were only paid for successful completion the first time. Second, when faculty who had completed the workshop were asked why they did not build *more* online and hybrid courses after the workshop, they answered that they wanted an incentive such as a stipend. And third, there were faculty who wanted more than a skills update. They wanted advanced skills training and pedagogy, and they wanted it in a convenient and effective format.

In order to stay within the CHSS policies compensating faculty for high quality course development while at the same time responding to faculty requests and fostering the development of more online and hybrid courses, 3 directors of distance learning and 10 online coordinators from CHSS designed and created a pilot training program for advanced users to develop online courses. The alpha version of this program was termed "The Project." This training consisted of a series of learning modules developed and designed to offer participants with existing teaching experience a program for advanced instructional development.

At the same time, data was drawn as part of an action research project to extend faculty professional development literature. Torbert's (2004) *developmental action inquiry* was chosen to facilitate participant self-transformation as well as enhance instructor creativity, awareness, justness and sustainability and guide data collection over the course of the program. Using the developmental action inquiry framework, data was collected in two ways: First, at the end of each learning module, the discussion board postings were reviewed for insights regarding the effectiveness of the module. Second, each participant completed a 15-item survey related to "The Project" at the end of the training program (see Appendix A).

Results

"The Project" was initiated by the Director of Distance Education in the College of Humanities and Social Sciences at Kennesaw State. The purpose of "The Project" was to create advanced online professional development to provide faculty within HSS at KSU who already teach online with advanced tools and pedagogy to improve existing and future online courses. "The Project" focused on the development of online modules created and run by online coordinators, alpha tested by the developers functioning as program participants. Online Coordinators were designated faculty within each academic department in the CHSS at KSU who acted as a liaison between department faculty and the Office of Distance Education (ODE) in the College. Online coordinators in CHSS were responsible for supporting distance education in online, hybrid, and traditional classroom settings within their departments. This support was provided in the form of one-on-one sessions to brainstorm and troubleshoot distance learning issues with full-time and part-time faculty and included department-level training for instructional technology. The designated faculty received a supplemental stipend for assuming the additional responsibilities described above.

A total of 11 modules were created, 10 by the online coordinators and 1 by the Director of Distance Education. The Online coordinators were given freedom to select their own module topic with the guidelines that it should pertain to best practices and sharing knowledge and expertise relating to online learning, and that it should contain 30 minutes to an hour worth of content on their topic along with an interactive activity. Each participant was expected to log in each week and access the module contents and participate in the activities. Each module designer was expected to monitor his or her own module during the week that it was active and to provide feedback to participants.

The modules created by the Online Coordinators fell into one of four types: (1) pedagogy/online teaching, (2) trends, (3) technology, and (4) tips or lessons learned relating to the online coordinator position. The following are a list of the topic titles: Latest Research into Successful Online Learning; Best Practices in Mobile Learning, Faculty Presence in Online Courses, Get Your Students Heads into the Clouds!, Cloud Computing at Kennesaw State University, Strong and Effective Types of Feedback for Students in an Online Environment, Taking the Long View, How Online Learning Has Changed at Kennesaw State, Lessons Learned: Five Tips I Would Share with New Online Coordinators, Creative Assignments in the Online Classroom: The Virtual Museum, Learner-Content Interaction in Online Courses, Real Online Programs of Kennesaw State University, and The Use of Social Media in Online Teaching.

The design of the modules and the presentation of content varied depending on the module creator; however, each module was created to QM Standards in order to model best practices. Most online coordinators used voiceover PowerPoint to deliver their content (*Figure 1*), and two used a PowerPoint with more detailed notes. Some module designers had supplemental or required readings. Every module started with module objectives (*Figure 2*).

Every module also had a discussion board where participants were asked to reflect and interact by answering one or two directed questions relating to the material covered. Often participants were asked to relate their own experiences and methods of achieving a particular objective, such as establishing instructor presence in an online course (*Figure 3*).

This activity sometimes involved asking participants to provide examples from their own courses for all participants to be able to view and from which they could benefit (*Figure 4*).

Content comprehension and retention were verified in some modules by using self-assessment quizzes and drag and drop exercises (*Figures 5 and 6*).

Advanced Faculty Professional Development for Online Course Building: An Action Research Project

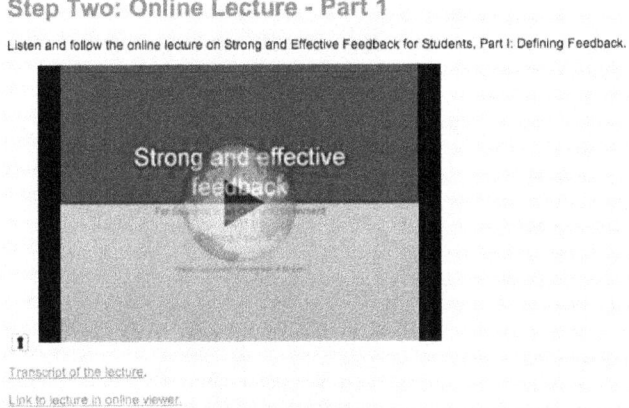

Figure 1. Voiceover PowerPoint Presentation

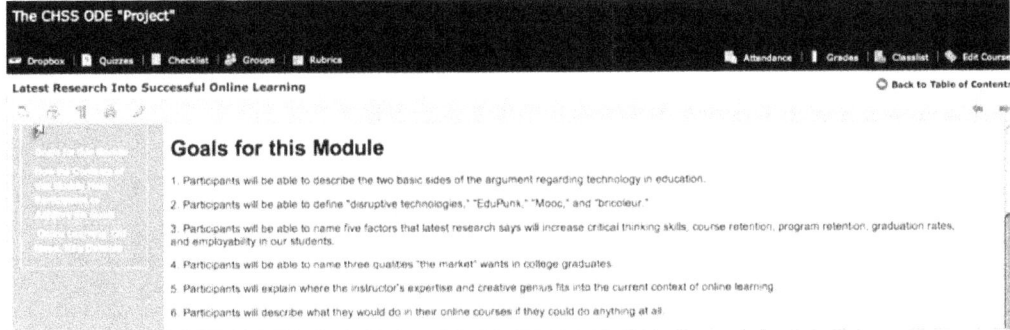

Figure 2. Module Objectives

Figure 3. Participant Experience Sample

Activity 3: Policies
12 messages - 0 unread

All:

'Copy & Paste' the statements / policies from your online class that describe your availability, email response time, grading turnaround time, etc., and feel free to describe your philosophy about these issues in your post and/or comment constructively on what others have submitted.

Figure 4. Request for course content sample

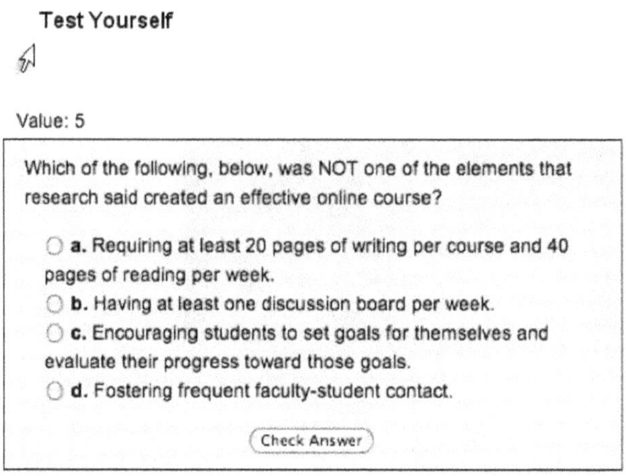

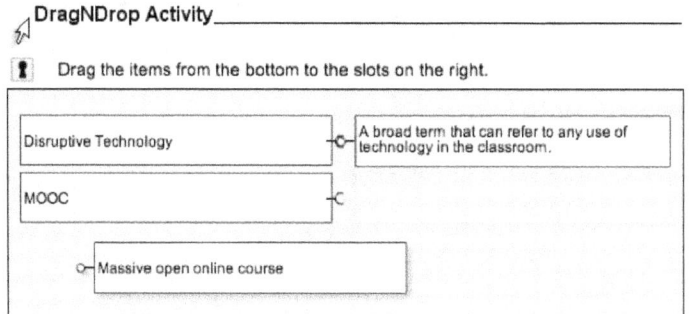

Figure 5. Self-assessment Quiz

Figure 6. Drag-N-Drop Exercise

Since the professional development offered in "The Project" was completely centered on these online modules, a learning management system was employed to deliver the content. The modules were hosted on Desire2Learn. Each module was opened to participants on Tuesday, and it was expected that all participants would complete that module by the following Monday evening at midnight.

Discussion

The lessons learned from this action research project were interpreted from a review of the learning module discussion boards and the responses provided to the 15-item survey administered after completion of "The Project." For example, the Online Coordinators were asked how they felt about "The Project" before it started and after it was completed. While only 20% stated they were enthusiastic about "The Project" before it started, 50% were enthusiastic about it after it ended. The majority of participants (60%) stated that the pedagogy/online teaching modules were the most helpful to them. The following sections highlight additional salient themes based on a quantitative and qualitative analysis of the data. These themes are presented in three conceptual categories including concern regarding time given to complete the modules, the feeling of success, and the need for revision.

Category 1: Faculty voiced concern with how long it took to complete modules.

When introduced to the idea of "The Project," a leading concern for most of the faculty involved the time needed to complete the modules and to create their individual modules. One participant voiced this concern in a response to survey item 1, "Given increasingly large loads and tenure-related expectations, the number one concern was time. I did, however, learn a lot about online teaching and distance learning so the extra effort was worth it." This concern for the amount of time it would take to participate in the learning modules and create a module may have also impacted the participants' level of enthusiasm upon beginning work on "The Project." Initially, 50% of the participants reported feeling "neutral" with regards to completing "The Project."

Category 2: Faculty found advanced training beneficial and timely.

Several of the participants indicated that the project can potentially be used for "faculty development and community-building among colleagues." Specifically, they enjoyed reading the experiences of other online teachers and coordinators, and they appreciated the online delivery of "The Project." Multiple participants commented on "the variety of the modules," indicating they were able to gather new information related to a spectrum of topics as presented in the individual learning modules. In particular, 60% of the participants appreciated the modules that focused on the pedagogy of online teaching, while 30% valued the technology-based modules.

It is also important to note that upon completing the learning modules presented in "The Project," the level of enthusiasm had increased significantly from the 50% reported initially. After completion, 90% of the participants reported feeling "somewhat enthusiastic" or "enthusiastic," while only 10% remained "neutral." Perhaps most importantly, 90% of the participants reported they were better online teachers after completing "The Project," and 70% reported they were better online coordinators. One participant referenced this apparent change in the way he or she viewed "The Project," "Once I started seeing the very interesting contributions, I thought it was brilliant."

Category 3: Faculty identified what needed revision in the program.

Although there were several successes experienced throughout the implementation of "The Project" and everyone referenced the potential benefit of its activities, there was also an obvious need for revisions of several of the components. One participant reported, "I see potential for this, but it needs refinement." One constant theme among the needed revisions relates to the consistency and quality of the learning modules. The following suggestions taken from the end-of-project survey reference the disparity that existed among the modules:

- "It needs to be put together as a more consistent product. Some of the modules will not work for this purpose -- those should be removed. Additional modules with technology (how to use some of the tools addressed in the other modules) should be added."
- "Some modules were better developed than others. Also, discussion boards alone don't reflect good practice in my opinion."

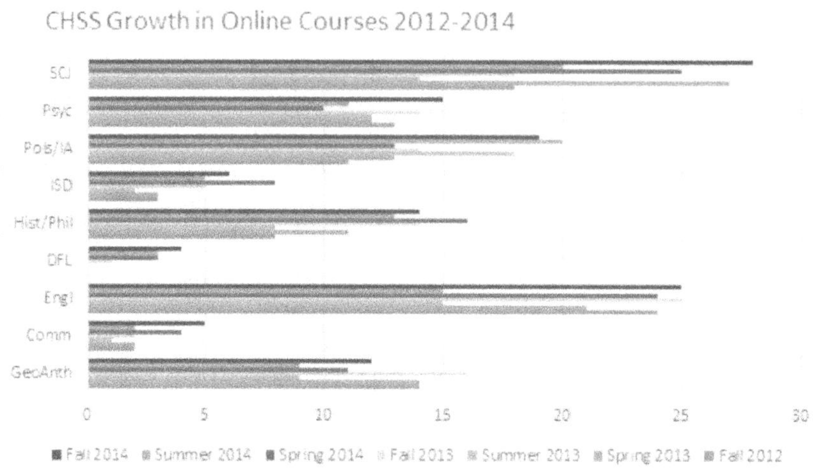

Figure 7. CHSS Growth in Online Courses 2012-2014
   Legend:
   SCJ=Sociology and Criminal Justice
   Psyc=Psychology
   Pols/IA=Political Science and International Affairs
   ISD=Interdisciplinary Studies
   Hist/Phil=History and Philosophy
   DFL=Department of Foreign Languages
   Engl=English
   Comm=Communication
   Geo/Anth=Geography and Anthropology

Thirty percent of the participants expressed that Kennesaw State University Online Coordinator specific modules were not very helpful.

- "The quality of the modules varied too much. It seemed like there were a lot of modules. It would have been effective with fewer modules."

One participant called for providing more "clarity about what it ["The Project"] entails at the beginning." The question arose, is "The Project" intended for the development of technology skills or for advanced training to develop additional online courses?

Another participant suggested that the facilitators "build into this project various course assignments that relate to the required deliverable (a new course)." In this manner, the participants would hone their technology skills while developing a new online course. It is particularly encouraging to note that 80% of the survey respondents indicated that they would be willing to create additional modules.

Next Steps: Action Items of Research

Building on the aforementioned need for revisions, a subgroup of "The Project" reviewed the created modules and selected those most appropriate for *advanced* faculty development. Two online coordinators, the instructional designer, and the director of CHSS ODE then created software and pedagogy modules to increase the number of modules for advanced faculty development to 15. The program's final modules included:

(a) Softchalk,
(b) Best Practices in Mobile Learning,
(c) The Latest Research on Successful Online Learning,
(d) Strong and Effective Types of Feedback,
(e) Panopto,
(f) Get Your Students' Heads INTO the clouds: Cloud computing,
(g) Creative Assignments in the Online Classroom: The Virtual Museum,
(h) VoiceThread,
(i) "Faculty Presence" in Online Courses,
(j) Doceri: An iPad App for Creating Content "On the Go",
(k) Tiki Toki,
(l) Learner-Content Interaction in Online Courses,
(m) The Use of Social Media in Online Teaching,
(n) Work Smarter, Not Harder, and
(o) Wiki is Hawaiian for Fast!

With the modules set, faculty members were offered a chance to participate in the advanced faculty development program entitled "Skills Update Workshop". To promote the development of additional online courses, successful completion of this new training and the subsequent delivery of a new online course resulted in the awarding of a $1000 stipend to the faculty member, an amount consistent with the average recommendation of the online coordinators who completed the survey.

As *Figure 7* indicates, the "Skills Update Workshop" resulted in the creation of 25 new online courses since the program was first offered in fall 2012. The increases in online course offerings are presented based on departments in HSS.

While all HSS departments have not developed new online courses at the same rate, most departments have increased their online course offerings each successive year since 2012. Above all, ODE is now well positioned to meet its goal for additional online course offerings based on its faculty training programs refined through this and related research.

Summary

The benefits of faculty development for enhancing teaching effectiveness have been well documented (Emerson & Mosteller, 2000; Gillespie & Robertson, 2010); nevertheless, motivating faculty to pursue *advanced* faculty development opportunities presents a unique challenge in light of the increasing expectations and competing priorities. Given this challenge, the "The Project" was developed at Kennesaw State University to train faculty in online course development and delivery. Based on this and concurrent research examining "The Project" (Terantino, Slinger-Friedman, Thomas, Randall, Aust, & Powell, 2014; Slinger-Friedman, Terantino, Randall, Aust, & Powell, 2014), the resulting "Skills Update Workshop" has gone far in providing faculty members advanced technology training for online instruction at Kennesaw State.

The success of any faculty training program hinges on creating a program that effectively delivers appropriate content in a supportive environment. The findings of this research offer a roadmap for improving the content and structure of online instruction in new and existing online courses. In sum, this research describes one solution to the professional development of *advanced* faculty training for online teaching for faculty at Kennesaw State University and at institutions like it.

References

Allen, I. E., & Seaman, J. (2011). Going the distance: Online education in the United States, 2011. Needham, MA: Babson Survey Research Group. http://www.babson.edu/Academics/centers/blank-center/global-research/Documents/going-the-distance.pdf

Allen, I. E., & Seaman, J. (2013). Changing course: Ten years of tracking online education in the United States. Babson Survey Research Group and Quahog Research Group, LLC. http://www.onlinelearningsurvey.com/reports/changingcourse.pdf. OCLC 826867460

Allen, I. E., & Seaman, J. (2014). Grade level: Tracking online education in the United States. Babson Survey Research Group and Quahog Research Group, LLC. http://onlinelearningconsortium.org/read/survey-reports-2014/

Baran, E. & Correia, A. (2014). A professional development framework for online teaching. *TechTrends, 58*(5), 96-102.

Barker, A. (2003). "Faculty development for teaching online: Educational and technological issues." *Faculty Development for Teaching Online, 34*(6), 273-278. OCLC 110677197.

Betts, K. & Heason, A. (2014). Build it but will they teach?: Strategies for increasing faculty participation and retention in online and blended education. *Online Journal of Distance Learning Administration, 17*(11). http://www.westga.edu/~distance/ojdla/summer172/betts_heaston172.html

Cho, M., & Rathbun, G. (2013). Implementing teacher-centred online teacher professional development (oTPD) programme in higher education: A case study. *Innovations in Education and Teaching International, 50*(2), 144-156.

Cohen, L., Manion, L., & Morrison, K (2007). Research methods in education (6th ed.). New York, NY: Routledge.

Dede, M. Ketelhut, D. J., Whitehouse, P. Breit, L., & McCloskey, E. M. (2009). A research agenda for online teacher professional development. *Journal of Teacher Education, 60*(1), 8-19. Doi:10.1177/0022487108327554.

Emerson, John D., & Moesteller, F. (2000). Development programs for faculty: Preparing for the Twenty-First Century. *Educational Media and Technology Yearbook 25*: 26-42. OCLC 425068080.

Fink, L. D. (2003). Creating significant learning experiences. San Francisco, CA: Jossey-Bass.

Gillespie, K. J., & Douglas L. R. (Eds.). (2010). A Guide to Faculty Development (2nd ed.). San Francisco, CA: Jossey-Bass. OCLC 607555028.

Gregory, J. & Salmon, G. (2013). Professional development for online university teaching. *Distance Education, 34*(3), 256-270.

Healy, S., Block, M., & Judge, J. (2014). Certified adapted physical educators' perceptions of advantages and disadvantages of online teacher development. *Palaestra, 28*(4), 14-16.

Hermann, J. H., (2013). Faculty incentives for online course design, delivery, and professional development. *Innovative Higher Education, 38,* 397-410.

Institute on Rehabilitation Issues (2002). Distance education: Opportunities and issues for the public VR program. Report from the Study Group, 28th IRI. Washington, DC: George Washington University.

Lewin, Kurt. 1946. "Action research and *minority problems."* Journal of Social Issues, 2(4), 34-46, doi: 10.1111/j.1540-4560.1946. tb02295.x. OCLC 4651349205.

Lin, C. & Davidson, G. (1995). Effects of linking structure and cognitive style on students' performance and attitude in a computer-based hypertext environment. Paper presented at the National Convention of the Association for Education Communications and Technology, Nashville, TN.

Navarro, P. & Shoemaker, J. (1999). The power of cyberlearning: An empirical test. *Journal of Computing in Higher Education, 11*(1), 29-57. Doi.org/10.1007/BF02940841.

Nerlich, A. P., Soldner, J. L., & Millington, M. J. (2012). Inter-university collaboration for online teaching innovation: An emerging model. *Rehabilitation Research, Policy, and Education, 26*(4), 321-344.

Paulus, T. M., Carole, R. M., Mixer, S. J., Wyatt, T. H., Lee, D. S., & Lee, J. L. (2010). *For faculty, by faculty: A case study of learning to teach online.* Berkley Electronic Press. http://www.bepress.com/ljnes/vol7/iss1/art13 DOI: 10.2202/1548-923X.1979.

Roth, S. M. (2014). Improving teaching effectiveness and student learning through the use of faculty learning communities. *Kinesiology Review, 3,* 209-216. http://dx.doi.org/10.1123/kr.2014-0059

Shattuck, J. & Anderson, T. (2013). Using a design-based research study to identify principles for training instructors to teach online. *The International Review of Research in Open and Distance Learning.* http://files.eric.ed.gov/fulltext/EJ1017553.pdf

Slinger-Friedman, V., Terantino, J. Randall, C., Aust, P., & Powell, T. (2014). Refining Advanced Development for Online Teaching and Course Building: An Evaluation from the Faculty Perspective. *The International Journal on Advances in Life Sciences.* http://www.iariajournals.org/life_sciences/tocv6n34.html

Sujo de Montes, L. E., & Gonzales, C. L. (2000). Been there, done that: Teaching teachers through distance education. *Journal of Technology and Teacher Education, 8*(4), 351-371.

Sturner, K., Koning, K. D., Seidel, and T. (2013). Declarative knowledge and professional vision in teacher education. Effect of course in teaching and learning. *British Journal of Educational Psychology, 83,* 467-483.

Terantino, J., Slinger-Friedman, V., Thomas, G., Randall, C., Aust, P., & Powell, T. (2014). Faculty perceptions of "The Project": An advanced faculty professional development for online course building. Proceedings of The Sixth Conference on Mobile, Hybrid, and On-line Learning, eLmL, 2014, Barcelona, Spain. https://www.thinkmind.org/index.p?view=article&articleid=elml_2014_3_40_50059

Torbert, W. (2004). *Action Inquiry: The*

Secret of Timely and Transforming Leadership. San Francisco: Berrett-Koehler Publishers.

Torbert, W. (2002). *Learning to exercise timely action now in Leading, Loving, Inquiring, and Retiring.* E-publication available from the author torbert@bc.edu. http://www.williamrtorbert.com/

Wang, F. & Hannafin, M. J. (2005). Design-based research and technology-enhanced learning environments. *Educational Technology Research and Development, 53*(4), 5-23. Doi.10.1007/BF02504682.

Wildavsky, B., Kelly, A., & Carey, K. (2011). *Reinventing Higher Education: The Promise of Innovation.* Cambridge, MA: Harvard Education Press. OCLC 724096928

Appendix A

Question 1: What were your thoughts when you were first introduced to the idea of "The Project"?
Question 2: Before "The Project" began, please rate your enthusiasm for it.
Question 3: After completing "The Project," how enthusiastic are you about the experience?
Question 4: Do you believe that this workshop, with a few modifications to make content more specific to online faculty, will effectively serve faculty who have completed the "Build a Web Course" Workshop and desire more professional development?
Question 5: Do you like the fact that it was all online?
Question 6: What category of modules was most helpful to you?
Question 7: What category of modules was least helpful to you?
Question 8: After completing "The Project," do you believe that you are a better online teacher?
Question 9: After completing "The Project," do you feel that you are a better online coordinator?
Question 10: What did you like least about "The Project"?
Question 11: What did you like most about "The Project"?
Question 12: What changes would you make to better serve your faculty who enroll in "The Project" pilot in fall?
Question 13: If asked, would you participate in creating another module for a similar endeavor such as "The Project"?
Question 14: How much should faculty be paid to complete "The Project" in a semester (not creating modules, just attending/participating)?
Question 15: What else would you like to share? Do you have any ideas for research?

www.ingramcontent.com/pod-product-compliance
Lightning Source LLC
Chambersburg PA
CBHW081352040426
42450CB00016B/3415